5.4.78

There is no question that the general mood in America today supports equality as never before. The traditional Christian doctrine of a wife submitting to her husband's authority is one of the most difficult positions for modern evangelists to defend. Should absolute equality carry over into the relationship between husband and wife in Christian marriage?

Herbert and Fern Harrington Miles believe that it should, but not because of any reasons advanced by contemporary social movements. In fact, the Miles household practiced equality in marriage decades before it became fashionable in the secular world. As they put it, "this book is built around the concept that husband-wife equality is revealed in the Bible as the plan of God in creation". The authors give a comprehensive overview and interpretation of those passages of Scripture from the Old and New Testaments that support equality in marriage. Herbert and Fern do not dodge verses that have been used to support the husband's authority. Instead, they carefully study each of them and find further support for their interpretation. While the position they take may not be traditional, it is soundly biblical and evangelical in its formulation.

The authors then proceed to apply the principle of equality throughout the full range of marital activities. HUSBAND-WIFE EQUALITY will bring the kind of relationship that God originally designed for Christian marriage—respecting one another, complementing each other and fulfilling one another's needs.

HUSBAND-WIFE EQUALITY

HERBERT J. MILES
AND
FERN HARRINGTON MILES

FLEMING H. REVELL COMPANY
OLD TAPPAN, NEW JERSEY

Library of Congress Cataloging in Publication Data

Miles, Herbert Jackson,
    Husband-wife equality.

    Bibliography: p.
    Includes index.
    1. Marriage. 2. Sex in marriage. 3. Husband and wife. 4. Sex and religion. I. Miles, Fern Harrington, joint author. II. Title.
HQ734.M564   261.8′34′27   77-27283
ISBN 0-8007-0906-3

TO
OUR PARENTS
whose faith in God and respect for human dignity
laid the foundation for rich interpersonal relationships
in our own lives

Contents

PART III: SEXUAL EQUALITY

APPENDIX: WHAT DOES THE BIBLE SAY

Preface

This book is built around the concept that husband-wife equality is revealed in the Bible as the plan of God in Creation. Part I studies the broad, basic biblical passages and principles that call for husband-wife equality and examines the Bible passages that are often used to establish husband-authority/wife-submission as being scriptural. Part II deals with the application of husband-wife equality in domestic life, including such areas as roles, management of finance, in-law relationships, communication, busyness, and a chapter on do-it-yourself marriage counseling. Part III sets forth a Christian theology of sex, including the biblical concept of husband-wife sexual equality. This concept is then applied to husband-wife real-life situations, designed to assist couples in finding a meaningful solution to sex-related issues such as: masculinity, femininity, birth control, frigidity, impotence, sexual fulfillment after sixty, and keeping romance in marriage. An appendix containing a more detailed study of Bible passages concerning husband-wife equality and Scripture often quoted to support the wife-submission theory, as well as a Scripture index and reading list complete this book.

In recent years many new books on family life have been written by husband-wife teams as co-authors. This is good. However, too few, if any, have revealed the process by which the two completed the manuscript. We feel it would be helpful to the readers to know something about us and just how together we wrote *Husband-Wife Equality*, especially since it *is* a book on this important subject.

Herbert has preached and taught husband-wife equality for over forty-five years. After forty-two years of happy married life as equals, he became a widower. Fourteen months later through the infinite wisdom and leadership of God, he married Miss Fern Harrington, who had been a Southern Baptist missionary to the Chinese in the Orient for over thirty-five years. During our courtship period, husband-wife equality was discussed and agreed upon as a guiding concept for our marriage. Now, after experiencing the happiness which results when the concept of husband-wife equality is put into practice on a daily basis, we are ready to recommend without reservation this way of life for all married couples.

Our backgrounds are amazingly similar: childhood in a rural farm Christian home; graduate degrees from the same theological seminary; leadership experience in local churches (Herbert, a pastor, and Fern, a missionary developing new churches); and more than twenty years each as professors in church-related schools on a college level or above.

Our common background has made it easier to think as one, but our varied experiences have enriched the content. Herbert, as college professor of sociology, has done extensive research on the husband-wife relationship, and over twenty years as a marriage counselor has given him an awareness of the varied problems married couples face. Fern is the product of a home whose mother was honored as State Missouri Mother in 1964. Fern has spent most of her adult life immersed in Chinese culture which is traditionally famous for its emphasis on moral values and the importance of the family in society. As a seminary professor training Chinese youth for leadership roles in church-related vocations, she had many opportunities for counseling in personal problems.

Both of us share an interest in writing and have had experience in publication. Herbert has published three books on courtship and marriage, writes a column on "Courtship, Marriage, and the Family" in several weekly newspapers in southeastern states. He has also written numerous articles for denominational publications. Fern was chosen to write a mission study book for children (published in 1958), and had a major role in the production of a Chinese hymnal published in 1973 and its English version published in 1976. She, likewise, has contributed several articles to mission journals. Our common background, as reflected in our lifestyle, conservative theological position, and moderate approach toward social issues—as well as our interest in writing—have made it easy to work together on this book.

We have written it together. It is not merely a combining of an equal number of essays written separately. It is not a fifty–fifty product. We have both given 100 percent of ourselves to the task. The book is the result of the uniting, fusing, and blending of the spiritual and rational potential of our total personalities into one finished product. In the beginning we agreed on an outline. Most of the time Herbert took the initiative in writing the first draft of each chapter. Then together we read, reread, double-checked, and polished every chapter, every paragraph, every sentence. From beginning to end, we have spent much time together, discussing, reviewing, and praying for God's guidance. We've literally lived this book for fifteen months. It has been a happy, growing experience for both of us.

In the process we have read over twenty books together, with Fern reading aloud, stopping at intervals to discuss statements related to husband-wife equality. Although we may not agree with all of their concepts, we have been influenced by and are grateful for the recent writings defending husband-wife equality including: Nancy Hardesty, Paul K. Jewett, Letha Scanzoni, James H. Olthuis, Virginia R. Mollenkott, Anne Plunkett Rosser, Jean Stapleton, Richard Bright and Dennis Guernsey. Although we do not agree with those who have written to establish husband-authority/wife-submission as being biblical, we have appreciated the recent writings of Larry Christenson, Elisabeth Elliot, Jack R. Taylor, Marabel Morgan, Ed and Gaye Wheat, Tim Timmons, Gladys Hunt, and Tim and Beverly LaHaye (to name a few). Their honesty, sincerity, and depth of Christian character is obvious. God bless them!

We gratefully acknowledge our indebtedness to dozens of people who have made valuable contributions to the writing of this volume. We are most indebted to Charles C. Hobbs, husband, father, clergyman, and college professor of English; and to Mrs. Jo Ann Spees, homemaker, mother, and teacher of English; both read the entire manuscript and made many excellent suggestions. Also, we are grateful to Dan Taylor, Bible and Greek professor, Jan Marie Addington and Gary E. Farley, sociologists, who made valuable suggestions. We express sincere thanks to college students Shirley Patterson and Becky Hobbs McCown for typing the manuscript during the early stages. Our special thanks go to high-school sophomore, Bonnie Vanaman, who typed the final manuscript.

HERBERT J. MILES

FERN HARRINGTON MILES

Carson-Newman College
Jefferson City, TN 37760

PART I

BIBLICAL EQUALITY

1

Introduction: A Committee of Two Has No Chairman

I (Herbert) will never forget the first time I officiated at a wedding ceremony. I was a junior in college and pastor of a rural church, preaching there the first Sunday in each month. A young couple, members of the church, Clarence Cleeton and Ella Pulis, made plans for me to perform their wedding ceremony. The date was set and the couple came to the house of my parents on Saturday afternoon for the ceremony. My parents, my brother and sister were witnesses. Since it was my first wedding, I had done my homework and was well prepared.

The ceremony was performed in solemn dignity. After the couple had been congratulated, the legal papers signed, and they had gone their happily married way, my father said, "Son, I want to ask you a question. Why did you require the bride and the groom to take different vows?" Smiling, he both kidded and scolded me, saying, "It seems to me you were easy on the groom but rather rough on the bride!" (To the groom I had said, "Do you promise to love, honor, cherish, and protect?" and to the bride I had said,

"Do you promise to love, honor, cherish, and obey?") I told him I had followed the standard minister's manual.

He said, "Maybe you should consider having a couple both take the same vows in your ceremonies!" My father, an honest, hardworking northeast Missouri farmer, had only an eighth-grade education and was not versed in theology. Yet the idea of requiring the wife to obey the husband puzzled him as being unfair.

My father's chiding me and his pertinent and stinging suggestion wounded my youthful pride, but it lingered in my mind and remained there, defiantly challenging the preconceived notion that I, without serious study or reflection, had picked up from the culture. As the weeks passed into months, I dug deeply into biblical and theological teaching about husband-wife relationships. My findings led me, in all honesty, to reverse my opinion. The word *obey* was deleted from my wedding ceremony. The decision did not come easily, because of the current religious opinion of that day, which believed and preached that the husband was the authority in the home and the wife was to be submissive to her husband. Through the years—in graduate school, in my pastoral ministry, and in twenty-three years of teaching on the college level in the areas of courtship, marriage, and family life—I have examined, investigated, checked, and double-checked the biblical teaching of the husband-wife relationship. Biblical, theological, and sociological evidence, in my opinion, affirms without exception the position of my rural father.

The Problem Stated

In recent years there has been a proliferation of Christian books which defend the concept of the husband's authority over the wife. No doubt this is an effort to stem the tide produced by the Women's Liberation Movement. We respect their sincerity and share their alarm. What bothers us, however, is the way they use isolated proof texts from the

Bible to defend their position. We feel this concept has its roots in our culture rather than the creative plan of God.

We live in a male-oriented society, which has traditionally accepted the authority of the husband in the family as normative. This concept, often described as "patriarchal," goes back to primitive society. Unfortunately many well-meaning Christians have accepted this point of view without making a serious study of the Scriptures to see if the Bible, as a whole, really does teach this as the ideal.

Many able, sincere Christian leaders promote this view. They insist the family must follow a God-ordained order, a chain of command, in which Christ is the head of the husband, the husband is the head of the wife and chief authority over the children.[1] Only then can the family (and therefore society) function properly. This assumed God-ordained order of authority is often referred to as the "hierarchy" doctrine; that is, an order in which each rank is subordinate to the one above it. For convenience, we will use the term *hierarchy* to refer to the male-dominant concept.

The main purpose of this book is to show that the Bible teaches husband-wife equality, and that the hierarchy concept is in conflict with broad, basic, universal biblical principles and truths.

Our Theological Point of View

The title of this book may come under the heading of "Fools Rush In Where Angels Fear to Tread." On the other hand, as Abraham Lincoln once said, "To sin by silence when they should protest, makes cowards out of men."

In our effort to establish husband-wife equality as being biblical, some readers may rather quickly identify us as being in the current stream of both liberal theology and the Women's Liberation Movement. Therefore, we will state our point of view concerning both movements now, in order to clear the air, before stating our case for husband-wife equality.

It is the part of wisdom for a speaker or author to state openly his general assumptions, rather than through sly trickery try to sneak them into the back door of his listener's or reader's mind—when he does not have the courage to bring them in the front door! Our concept of husband-wife equality is a deduction from our evangelical point of view. It includes the following:

1. The Bible has God as its Author, salvation for its end, and truth without any mixture of error, for its message. It is the supreme standard by which all human behavior, attitudes, and opinions should be judged.
2. There is only one living and true God. He is the personal, eternal triune God who is Creator, Redeemer, Sustainer, and Ruler of the universe. He is infinite in all qualities, including holiness. He reveals Himself to us as Father, Son, and Holy Spirit without division of His nature or person.
3. Jesus Christ, the eternal Son of God, was born of a virgin; revealed in His flesh the perfect will of God; died on the cross to redeem mankind from sin; was raised from the dead; ascended back to the Father and will return in power and glory to judge the world and complete His redemptive mission.
4. The Holy Spirit is the Spirit of God who inspired men to write the Scriptures. He exalts Christ; helps men and women to understand truth; and His presence in the Christian leads the believer and the church, in worship, evangelism, and service.
5. Man and woman were both created in the image of God and given freedom of choice. All have sinned against God and as sinners come under God's condemnation. Only through God's plan of grace, personal repentance, and faith in Christ can mankind find salvation and return

to their original relationship with God.

6. A New Testament church is a local group of baptized believers who observe the two ordinances (Baptism, and the Lord's Supper); associate in a covenant of faith and fellowship in Christ; and seek to extend the Gospel to all people in all nations.

7. God instituted marriage at the beginning of His creation of the human race and designed it to involve the total lifelong commitment of a man and woman to God and to each other.

8. In Christian marriage husband and wife become one, spiritually, intellectually, emotionally, socially, and physically. They function interdependently as equals. They are joint heirs with Christ and share equally in marriage joys and sorrows, and in decisions and responsibilities.

This we believe.

An Evaluation of the Women's Liberation Movement

The Women's Liberation Movement, like all human social movements, has both good and bad qualities. Some of its qualities which we believe to be more acceptable are: (1) It seems to be calling for equality, freedom, and democracy. (2) It opposes a patriarchal society. (Any student of history knows that patriarchal societies have gravely mistreated women, relegating them to the status of inferior, second-class citizens, and often to semi-slavery.) (3) It calls for equal pay for equal work. (There is growing concern over the fact that women receive much less pay than men for the same work performed.) [2] (4) It seems to insist that women should improve their self-images. (Both men and women could improve at this point.) (5) It points out that many wives have an adjustment problem during the "empty-nest" period when all the children have left and have their own homes. (This is a problem for some women, and it needs to be studied carefully.)

Almost everybody would agree that these concerns are justified. However, we are persuaded that when we have seen these ideas, we have seen only the tip of an otherwise ugly and dangerous iceberg. The Women's Liberation Movement has many serious weaknesses. Its writings, including those of Betty Friedan (beginning with *The Feminine Mystique*), Gloria Steinem, et al, are saturated with many small part-truths and false assumptions. They continually repeat the idea that most housewives are unhappy and bored, with little scientific evidence to support their claim. They insist that society has imprisoned women in the home by not allowing them freedom for self-development. They seem to assume that the only way a woman can have freedom and self-development is to pursue a professional career. They seem to assume that women must have a private personal destiny and identity apart from family life in order to be successful, to be happy, and to have normal self-fulfillment. They assume that motherhood and housework is not a career, and, therefore, cannot bring self-fulfillment to a woman. They seem to ignore the plan of the Creator in nature, namely, that only women have children and nurse them, and that men are stronger physically than women. They seem to forget that mothers, fathers, children, homes, mature family relationships are the building blocks of society and are the necessary foundation for preparing all of us for self-fulfillment. To be objective, it must be said that while they assume concern for mothers and homemakers, they proceed to diminish the importance of these roles by indicating that they are very limited.

Read their writings and note how they seldom refer to the word *love,* either between husband and wife or parents and children. They often seem to be more concerned about legalized abortion than they are about children. They seem to ignore the possibility that legalized abortion encourages immorality. They seem to assume that only homemakers have psychological problems and fail to notice that some of their own group are aggressive, social misfits, meandering between family life and the business and economic world—often succeeding in neither.

They fail to call attention to the hundreds of women who, although they have pursued a successful career in singleness and have had many scholastic and professional honors, have had in later life a heavy feeling of loneliness and incompleteness. These women eventually come to admit that they have neglected the one thing that means the most to a woman—that of being a wife and mother. They often spend these later years longing for the loving arms of a husband and little child. And we fear the Women's Liberation Movement ignores many mothers of their group, who neglected their husbands and children, and in later years were crushed by guilt feelings due to their personal neglect of their wife and motherhood responsibilities. To pursue successfully both dedicated motherhood and a busy career—and excel in both of them—requires either a woman of exceptional ability or a very unique situation indeed.

The Women's Liberation Movement, through the use of the propaganda media, keeps repeating, like a broken record, that housewives and mothers are unhappy. Some have begun to believe this false doctrine. A woman's purpose in life should come from within herself in the form of an urgent sense of duty and responsibility—with overtones of divine leadership—and not from endless repetition from a small, sophisticated clique, who often have a broken social and family-life experience. The Women's Liberation Movement seems to isolate and emphasize woman in a vacuum. We want to exalt and emphasize woman in a context of human relationships and Christian equality.

We wish to state unequivocally that we have no connection with the Women's Liberation Movement, nor has our social thinking or Christian philosophy been influenced by it. Herbert was teaching husband-wife biblical, domestic, and sexual equality long before the Women's Liberation Movement came into being.

The Case for Equality Stated

How are husbands and wives to think of each other? Who is the authority in the family? Who should make family decisions? What is the Bible's teachings concerning male and female? What does the Bible have to say about husband-wife roles and relationships? How should we relate cultural change to God's purposes for husband and wife? How should Christians today understand male-female, husband-wife relationships? Is "husband/authority-wife/submission" or "husband-wife equality" taught in the Bible? What is the meaning of husband-wife equality? These questions are intelligent. They need intelligent answers. They need Christian answers based on biblical truth.

The patriarchal doctrine (the husband is authority over the wife) was widely practiced among all preliterate peoples. It was practiced by the ancient Greeks, Romans, Hindus, Chinese, and Hebrews. While practice of ancestor worship helped to crystalize the practice of the patriarchal family, it is noteworthy that the Hebrews rejected ancestor worship. Practically all the European and Asiatic peoples were practicing as the patriarchal family when they first appeared in history. In many cases where patriarchies existed, the authority of the father and husband was so great that his wife and children were considered to be his property.

It may be somewhat easier for all of us to understand the emphasis on husband-dominance and wife-submission when we take a look at this history. In the past, the social world has been largely a world where authority and power over society was assumed, directed, and controlled by men. Concerning this, W. O. Carver says:

> The Christian church arose in a man's world and its men thought largely in terms of masculine responsibility and dominance. The Christian movement was expanded through the centuries into regions and cultures which were controlled by men who subordinated and dominated women. Thus almost universally men have applied and women have accepted in the churches the social standards and conventions of the communities in which the churches arose . . . . Men were the interpreters of the terms of the New Testament and expositors of the Christian principles. A too masculine cast has been given to the interpretations and expositions . . . . All translations of the Christian Scriptures reflect the warped viewpoints of man-controlled institutions in passages dealing with women . . . .[3]

An example of this is the prayer of Orthodox Jews who pray, "Blessed are you, Lord our God . . . who hath not created me a heathen . . . a slave . . . a woman." Many of the great intellectuals of the past have taught that God or Nature created man to rule over woman in the home and in society. This group would include Aristotle, Augustine, Thomas Aquinas, Schopenhauer, Rousseau, Sigmund Freud, Martin Luther, John Calvin, Zwingli, and many others.

This same patriarchal thought is easily read into the Bible today as being the divine will of God. For example, Ephesians 5:22–24 contains the following three statements: (1) "Wives be subject to your husbands . . ." (verse 22), (2) "The husband is the head of the wife . . ." (verse 23) and, (3) ". . . let wives also be subject in everything to their hus-

bands" (verse 24). Unfortunately, many well-meaning
Christians and devout Christian scholars have used these
and other similar passages as proof that husbands should
exercise authority over wives and that wives should be
submissive to their husbands.

The careful Bible reader should note three things about
this interpretation of the quotations above (Ephesians
5:22–24): (1) Each quotation is only a part of a larger sentence; (2) the interpretation is lifted out of the total context
of the passage (Ephesians 5:1–33); and (3) the interpretation
is in violation of broad, basic biblical truth.

After a careful study of biblical and sociological evi-
dences concerning male-female and husband-wife relationships, we are compelled to accept the concept of husband-
wife equality and to reject the hierarchy concept of
"husband/dominant-wife/subordinate" (sometimes called
"husband/dominant-wife/submission") doctrine. The hus-
band/dominant-wife/subordinate doctrine teaches that in
creating male and female, God created a divine *order* or
hierarchy in which the husband is the authority in the family and responsible for it. He is the head of the wife. The
wife lives under the authority of her husband and must be
subordinate and submissive to him. This is conscientiously
believed by many fine, sincere, scholarly Christians. They
are quick to point out that an authoritative husband and a
submissive wife does not mean that the husband is
superior and the wife inferior. But we cannot accept this
explanation. If language and words have meaning, it would
of necessity follow that, if the wife is to submit to the husband's authority, and be subordinate to him, he would be
superior and she would be inferior. Subordinate means
"belonging to a lower or inferior class or rank."

Some who advocate woman submission say that husband
and wife are fully equal on the spiritual level in all of their
relationships to God, but the woman is subordinate on the
level of family interpersonal relationships. This amounts to

two sets of divine standards, working at cross-purposes. It reminds us of some of the early attitudes towards slavery in America. They argued that the slaves were equals to the white man on the spiritual level, but on the social level they must be subordinate to the white man and kept "in their place."

Some also say the Bible teaches male-female equality but not husband-wife equality. If male and female are equal, on what basis does God give the husband authority over the wife? We find no justification for this distinction.

Others have said women *want* their husbands to have authority over them. It's true some women do extol the joys of so-called real or total submission. But this may be a cop-out. When the husband makes all the decisions, the wife is relieved of personal responsibility for wrong decisions. We feel the wife should share the burden of family decision making.

The Declaration of Independence states in the second paragraph that "all men [persons] are created equal." This does not mean that all people are alike. Each person, however, is a distinctive individual of worth. It does mean that decisions at every level in society are made by a democratic process. We Americans accept this and insist upon it in our national institutions and most of our churches. Yet many of our most sincere Christians insist that democracy will not work in the home between husband and wife. How can this be when people of all cultures agree that the family is the basic unit of society and civilization?

Some insist there must be a single authority in the family. They often say facetiously, "Who ever heard of an army with two heads?" But a family is not an army. A family of husband, wife, and children is a social institution created by God. An army is a social institution created by man. To say that since so-and-so is true of the army, it must also be true of the family is like adding apples and elephants. The final authority in the family is neither the husband nor the wife nor both. God is the final authority in the family.

To be fair, we must say those who follow the authority-submission theory go on to emphasize that the husband should *love* his wife, should avoid becoming a dictator or "lording" it over her. As a matter of fact, both those who advocate the authority-submission theory and the husband-wife equality theory actually end up largely describing husband-wife relationships in the same language. For example, they both say that neither husband nor wife is superior or inferior, that husbands should not lord it over their wives as selfish tyrants, and they both reject the idea of a balanced 50–50 relationship between husband and wife.

But the hierarchy thinkers often contradict themselves. One writer insists that the husband is the authority, the head of the wife, and the wife is to be subordinate and submissive to him. Then he insists that in a Christian home, submission should be mutual, both husband and wife yielding to the needs of the other. He is saying they are both equals but at the same time the husband is authority and the wife must be submissive—the husband is dominant and the wife is subordinate. Another writer insists that Paul calls on all parties to submit to each other in appropriate ways. He thinks that submission of each to the other in right attitudes creates a Christian atmosphere, and that this kind of mutuality can, and should, be beautiful. Then he contradicts himself by insisting that the wife should find it easy to revere and be subject to her husband.

Still another writer insists that it must be emphasized that as persons every member of a family is equal, but the wife is to subject herself to the leadership role of her husband. This is double-talk. It is like talking about a hot cold day, a tall short man, or a straight crooked line. It is calling white, black. This is a classic example of how emotional feelings of biblical scholars can blind their eyes to the truth. Actually the only difference between the two sides is that one insists on saying the husband is the authority (and therefore the

head of the wife) and the wife must be submissive and subordinate to her husband. The other side rejects this and
insists that husband and wife are "equals."

But this difference is major. It is great. It is serious. Carried to logical conclusions the difference leads in opposite
directions. If we carefully follow the logical consequences
and outgrowth of these two theories, we would come to the
realization that the authority-submissive idea tends to lead
us into personal, family, and social problems, while the
equality idea tends to lead us into interpersonal relationships that promote personality development, personal
fulfillment, happiness in marriage, a united family life, and a
progressive society.

A Definition of Equality

What do we mean by "equality" of husband and wife?
We do not mean a 50–50 relationship! Certainly not! We are
talking about 100 percent–100 percent relationship. We
mean that God, in creating male and female in His image,
created them on the nonphysical level, alike in nature,
status, value, worth, duties, opportunities, and responsibilities. Stated another way, God established in creation a
husband-wife relationship in which freedom and independence are equal, dependence and trust are mutual, and responsibility and reliability are reciprocal. On the level of
male and female experience, equality is a state of mind, an
attitude; it's an inner feeling that both should see themselves and each other as needing one another, complementing each other, and having the potential of fulfilling one
another's needs as persons, according to the divine plan set
forth in their being created in the image of God.

It is obvious that husband and wife have some biological
differences. The husband is physically stronger than the
wife and his sex drive appears on the surface to be exceedingly strong. Only the wife can have babies and nurse them.
(In spite of these differences, male and female are fantasti-

cally alike physically in many ways.) Therefore, in the marriage relationship they must of necessity play some different social roles in the family and society some of the time. However, this does not repeal or abolish their equality.

Thus, husband and wife are in a parallel mutual relationship of unity and equality in which each behaves toward the other in love, in grace, in privilege, and in spiritual joy as a person of worth. They are equals in self-surrender and devotion to each other. They are both leaders. They are both followers. They are both authority. They are both submissive. They are both dominant. They are both subordinate. They are both protectors. They are both spiritual and physical partners in a "one-flesh" unity that is a two-way street. They are "subject to one another" out of reverence for Christ.

A committee of two has no chairman.

2

Biblical Teachings About Husband-Wife Equality

Before examining the biblical concept of equality, we need to sketch some generally accepted standards of Bible interpretation. The following guidelines should be helpful.

Guidelines for Bible Interpretation

1. The Bible is a divine book, a message from God inspired by the Holy Spirit.
2. The Bible is a coherent unit giving principles, relationships, and interests concerning God's redemptive love in Christ.
3. The Bible is an historical book, written by man, reflecting human ideas and cultures. This in no way invalidates the divine nature of the book, just as the divinely inspired nature of the Bible in no way invalidates its historical human nature.
4. We need to distinguish between the revealed will of God and the cultural traditions and practices of the society in which each book of the Bible was written.
5. Passages that are positive, theological, and doctrinal in context and content, should be used to interpret those passages dealing with the cultural and social customs of the day.
6. All parts of the Bible should be interpreted in light of (a) the meaning of the author; (b) the context of each paragraph; and (c) the context of the broad, basic principles

of God's purpose in the entire Bible.

7. In the process of revealing Himself and His will through the Jewish nation, God often had to allow human practices of a culture that were in conflict with His will. This was necessary in order to get His divine purposes established and at the same time respect the freedom of persons involved—in this case—Hebrews. An example would be that God permitted polygamy among the Jews for a while in order to reveal that monogamy was His plan for marriage.

8. Christians should be careful about building doctrinal systems on a few isolated passages whose meanings tend to be fuzzy and unclear.

Positive Doctrinal Statements

The Bible teaches that both male and female were created in the image of God, and therefore that husband and wife are in a relationship of equality (Genesis 1:27; 5:1–2). It calls for a man to *leave* his father and mother and *cleave* to his wife and the two should become one flesh (Genesis 2:24). This describes unity and equality. The Bible teaches that Jehovah God authorized both Adam and Eve (husband and wife) to be equally responsible for the task of populating the earth and ruling over the rest of creation (Genesis 1:28). The Bible teaches that men and women are equals as sinners before God (Romans 3:23) and are equals in the process of receiving God's grace in salvation and in eternal life (John 3:16; 1 Peter 3:7).

Paul taught that husbands and wives are equals in sexual needs and in sexual rights, each depending on the other and each meeting the other's sexual needs (1 Corinthians 7:2–5). He also taught that men and women (husbands and wives) are social equals in the Christian family and community (Ephesians 5:21). Therefore, all sex discrimination should cease since males and females are equals in Christ (Galatians 3:28). Furthermore, even though woman was created from Adam's rib, and all men owe their existence to being born of women, both equally owe their existence to God (1 Corinthians 11:11, 12). Following the teachings of Jesus (Matthew 18:14), Paul called for equality when he taught that Christian humility calls for all people to count others (whether husband or wife) better than themselves (Philippians 2: 3, 4). Paul's relationships to women indicated he thought of men and women as equals since he refers to women as "fellow laborers" and "co-workers" in the Lord (Romans 16:1, 3–6; Philippians 4:3).

The Fifth Commandment (Exodus 20:12) and the passage often called the Golden Rule includes both men and women and assumes their equality (Luke 6:31). Both men and women were accepted as believers (Acts 5:14) and were baptized (Acts 8:12). The life and teachings of Jesus as related to women indicated that He thought of women as equals to men, and He treated them as equals.

We submit that these positive, basic, doctrinal guideline passages from the Holy Scripture leave no room for authoritative husbands and subordinate wives.

The Hierarchy Basis for Wife-Submission

The hierarchy advocates begin their thinking by assuming in advance the patriarchal authority of husbands over wives and then religiously read this doctrine into a few Bible passages. These passages are largely those that reflect Paul's attempt to correct specific women who were practicing questionable behavior, often during worship services. This was an effort to protect the women and the churches from undue criticism, as new converts enjoyed their new-found freedom of equality with men, or from questionable behavior where new converts were unwisely holding on to some pre-Christian customs.

In studying the arguments used by the hierarchy thinkers, one is impressed with their honest determination to read husband/authority-wife/submission into the Scriptures.

They leave no stone unturned looking for evidence to undergird their theory. Yet, in spite of their determined effort, they tend to rest their case on a few selected passages such as Genesis 1:28–3:17; 1 Corinthians 11:3, 8, 9; 14:34–37; Ephesians 5:22–31; and 1 Timothy 2:11–14. It is unusual that they claim to present all the evidence of the Scriptures and are so determined to prove their case that they fail to apply the many basic passages that deal directly and positively with male-female/husband-wife equality to their doctrine of hierarchy (Genesis 1:26, 27; 2:25; 5:1, 2; Romans 3:23; John 3:16; 1 Peter 3:7; 1 Corinthians 7:2–5; Ephesians 5:21; Galatians 3:28; 1 Corinthians 11:11, 12; Luke 14:11; Romans 16:3; Philippians 4:3; Acts 8:12; and Luke 6:31). We would have to agree with Nancy A. Hardesty that "Everything the entire Bible has to say about human beings applies to women . . . ." [4]

A Careful Study of the Fifth Chapter of Ephesians

It may be that the fifth chapter of Ephesians is the most misunderstood chapter in the Bible. The husband-wife hierarchy concept of husband/authority–wife/submission or husband/dominant–wife/subordinate doctrine, which is assumed, is read into the chapter. Actually, Paul is calling for husband-wife equality in an effort to lead Christians out of the pagan patriarchal practices of husbands ruling over their wives and keeping them in near-slavery subjection. When approached without the assumed patriarchal hierarchy doctrine in mind, the basic meaning of chapter five is obvious. Let us carefully examine this passage in an effort to understand its teaching.

The first three chapters of Ephesians emphasize the reality of redemption in Christ. Paul states the total Gospel including: (1) Christ became flesh (2:15); (2) He died on the cross (2:16); (3) through His blood shed on the cross we are forgiven, reconciled, and redeemed (1:7); (4) Christ was raised from the dead (1:20); ascended back to the Father and pours out His grace to free us from sin (1:20); (5) He is the head of the universe (1:10); and, (6) He is the head of the church (the Christian community) throughout the world (1:21, 23).

In chapters 4 through 6, Paul describes the results of salvation in Christ to the Ephesians. He gives details on how they should live as Christians. Since the Ephesians were once Jews and Gentiles (5:8), but are now fellow Christians in Christ, they must be very careful how they live (5:8, 11). They must turn their backs on the old life of sin (4:17) and learn the new life in Christ (4:15). They must stop living in immorality like the Gentiles in Ephesus (5:3–6). They must live thoughtfully as wise Christians (5:15).

One should note that through Ephesians 5:20 Paul has said nothing about husband-wife hierarchy. From 4:1 to 5:20 he gives careful instructions on how the new Ephesian converts should live in Christ. Then in 5:21 Paul summarized his instructions in one short, simple, clear, and decisive statement: "Be subject to one another out of reverence for Christ." The word *subject* is a translation of the Greek *hupotasso*. *Hupo* means *under* and *tasso* means *to arrange*. It was originally a military term referring to the relation of a soldier to his commanding officer. Paul uses it in this passage to explain the relationships between Christians. It is best translated *relate yourselves to, respond to,* or *adjust yourselves to* one another out of reverence for Christ. No matter how it is translated, it means that all Christians should do it. It is something that Christians do to *one another*.

All Christians are to be subject to or relate themselves to all other Christians. It includes both male and female, both husbands and wives. The relationship is parallel and mutual. It is a two-way street. It is a universal, reciprocal relationship of Christians regardless of class, race, or sex. The husband-wife illustration (5:22–33) is simply saying that husbands should be subject to or respond to the needs of their wives and wives should be subject to or respond to the needs of their husbands out of reverence for Christ.

Verse 21 is the hinge connecting Ephesians 4:1–5:20 and Ephesians 5:22–6:9. The hinge on a gate is necessary for the gate to swing efficiently. A gate must be anchored to a solid post or foundation. Verse 21 is anchored in the solid, clear, positive statements of 4:1–5:20 that all converts should turn their back on sin and pagan behavior and live like Christians. Following verse 21, Paul gives three illustrations that are designed to explain and describe the meaning of verse 21. The three illustrations are: (1) husband-wife relations (5:22–33); (2) parent-child relations (6:1–4); and, (3) master-slave relations (6:5–9).

These three simple illustrations are the gate which opens up to the readers the meaning of verse 21. They are not isolated doctrines upon which we are to build an organized theological system, but are only illustrations of the positive biblical doctrine in verse 21. They each have the same meaning, namely, that all Christians should "subject themselves to (or relate themselves to) one another out of reverence for Christ." Every sentence, every phrase, and every word in these three illustrations must be interpreted in light of verse 21. To read the husband/dominant–wife/subordinate doctrine into verse 21 is in direct violation of verse 21 and of the total context involved. Although those who read the hierarchy concept into Ephesians 5:22–33 are sincere and honest Christians, it is misleading and false Bible interpretation.

The hierarchy thinkers always ask for an explanation of the term *submit* (or *be subject to*) in verse 22 and the term *head* in verse 23. The term *submit* has been discussed above. What does the term *head* mean when Paul says in verse 23, "For the husband is the head of the wife as Christ is the head of the church . . . "? Certainly it would be pressing the meaning of this verse too far—and would be taking it out of context—to say that the husband is the head of the wife in the *same sense* that Christ is the head of the church. How did Christ get to be the head of the church? He became the Savior and Lord of the church in that He died for it on the cross. Husbands have not died for the salvation of their wives. Certainly the word *head* does not mean that the husband has ownership of his wife with authority to impose his will on her, as our friends the hierarchy thinkers point out.

The meaning of the words *submit* and *head* can only be understood by laying the hierarchy assumption aside, and understanding these words in light of verse 21 and in light of the larger context of chapter 5 and Paul's entire letter—plus seeing these words against the background of the full equal love and respect to be shared by husband and wife. This equal love includes fusing of all of the manly qualities and potentialities of the husband, and all the womanly qualities and potentialities of the wife, into one flesh.

Those who read a rigid order and hierarchy into the terms *submit* and *head* overlook two other points. First, Paul gives only three and one-third verses about the wife's relation to the husband, but gives eight and two-thirds verses to outline the husband's relation to the wife. In the Greek language, the verbs used in describing the wife's relation to the husband do not use the imperative mode, but verbs in the imperative mode *are* used in describing the husband's relationship to the wife. A Greek verb in the imperative mode has the meaning of an obligatory act or duty, a rule, an order, or a command. Therefore, the greater responsibility and obligation in the marriage relationship seems to be placed upon the husband.

Second, note that in talking to husbands Paul changes from the word *submit* to the word *love*. Why? The answer is obvious. In that day, Greek wives were forced to stay at home and care for the children, were kept ignorant, had no social or political status, and were in semi-slavery. And worst of all, a wife was not loved by her husband. The husband's social and sex life was in association with Greek single young women, who were educated, but very immoral. For a Greek husband to love his wife in the sense of Christian love was an isolated exception. This is why Paul used such strong language (verses 25–33) in insisting that husbands love their wives. It was a definite effort to raise the level of the attitudes of the new Christian husbands toward their wives *from* the low level of inferior, inhuman degradation and debasement of women of the pagan world *to* husbands loving their wives in a Christian atmosphere of equality. Thus Paul's command for husbands to love their wives was a sudden and major change in the social structure of family life of that day.

When we consider that the pagan husbands of Ephesus were the dominating heads of their wives, and when we consider the cruel oppression of women by the ugly, sad, and sordid patriarchal system back through the pages of history, Paul's advice to husbands is a welcome breath of fresh air.

In order to understand the meaning of verses 22–23, we need to see the mechanics of Paul's husband-wife illustration used to depict the relationships all Christians should have for each other. The concept of *relationships* is the key to understanding this passage. His illustration compares the relationships of husband and wife to that of Christ and the church. We have four separate entities or concepts in the illustration, namely, husband, wife, Christ, church. The husband's Christian behavior relationship is compared to Christ's behavior as Savior, and the wife's Christian behavior relationship is compared to the church's behavior toward Christ. In this context Christ is authority over the church, but that is not what Paul is talking about. He is saying that Christ loved the church and related Himself to the church by giving Himself on the cross. Likewise, in this context, the church considers Christ as its authority and does submit to His leadership. But that is not what Paul is discussing. He is discussing how the church related itself to Christ. How? It loved Him and tried to relate itself to Him through love.

There is nothing in the fifth chapter of Ephesians that would even remotely indicate that (1) husbands are dominant and wives are subordinate; (2) that wives should submit to their husbands' decisions; (3) that husbands have final authority over their wives; or, (4) that wives are a secondary authority in the family. The chapter is *not discussing human rights or authority, for any individual.* It is discussing *Christian duties, obligations, and responsibilities,* for all individuals within the Christian fellowship. It is simply saying all Christians should relate themselves one to another out of reverence for Christ. This includes both husbands and wives. It calls for solidarity, union, and equality among all Christians everywhere. The ground is level at the cross.

(See *Appendix* for a more detailed study of Bible passages indicating husband-wife equality as well as Scriptures often quoted to support husband/authority–wife/submission theory.)

Husband~Authority / Wife~Submission

HIERARCHY

Husband

Wife

". . . You have been weighed in the balances, and found want-
ing" (Daniel 5:27).

Husband–Wife Equality

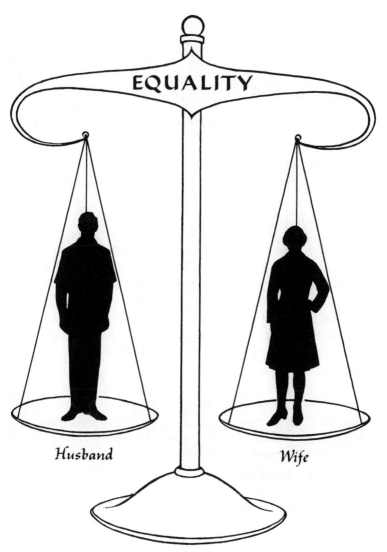

"Be subject to one another out of reverence for Christ"
(Ephesians 5:21).

3

The Advantages of Husband-Wife Equality

Husband-wife equality has many practical advantages and should produce positive fruits in their interpersonal relationships, in their family, and in the community.

Courtship

One of the major advantages of the doctrine of equality is the results that follow when it is applied in the courtship processes. In our male-oriented society the male-authority doctrine still overflows into courtship patterns. In many communities even today, boys are to take the initiative in courtship and girls are supposed to be coy and passive. They are not supposed to ask for a date. They are not supposed to propose. They are expected to sit quietly with folded hands and wait until they are asked. Some girls are seldom asked. A few are never asked. Thus they are locked into this cruel discriminating system. Many girls have said *yes* the first or second time asked lest they not be asked again. Often very poorly matched marriages are the result. If girls were given the opportunity to take the initiative in courtship the same as boys, they would have a fair chance to select the husband they want and need, with more assurance of a good marriage.

This one-sided courtship system is not a deduction from the will of God or basic Bible doctrines concerning male-female relationships. It is an unsocial, unchristian deduction from thousands of years of man-invented, man-promoted, man-enforced, self-appointed male authority, power, and supremacy. This is a wretched system and we propose that it be changed.

If girls were allowed to take the initiative in courtship in our society, what would be the positive results? Girls would have more social dates. This would help them to develop self-esteem. It would help bring an end to some long, lonely evenings while other young girls, who were asked, are having a pleasant time associating with other fine young people. It would lead to more marriages. Marriage is the plan of the Creator. It tends to foster a social and moral community. It would mean better marriages. In courtship, girls tend to look deeper than physical attractiveness, and thus would select a more compatible mate. On the other hand, boys, because of their intense sex drive, tend to seek the physically beautiful girl, the one that appeals to them sexually. Certainly physical beauty is a worthy consideration in selecting a marriage companion, but it should not be the first consideration and should not be the only consideration. Physical beauty alone is spurious and dangerous beauty. Some boys chase after the most beautiful girl in the community. Competition is fierce. Finally, a boy succeeds in marrying her, and six months later may find he is married to a selfish, lazy, discontented nag.

There are some girls in every community who are mature in mental, emotional, social, and religious traits, who might not win a Hollywood beauty contest. Yet when a boy dates one and through association gets acquainted with the total person and all of her fine qualities, she becomes the most beautiful girl he knows. If girls were allowed to take the initiative in courtship, they would have a wider selection and, as a result, we ought to have better marriages.

If girls could take the initiative in courtship, it would relieve some of the courtship expense for boys. Under our patriarchal system, boys are supposed to pay all of the courtship expense. Since the person asking for a date would pay for it, girls would pay when they asked. There are many boys who have to work their way through high school and college who would appreciate the girl's sharing in courtship expense. (Fortunately, in many parts of the country, this pattern is changing, and girls are starting to share the cost of dating.)

There are many timid boys. In light of the fact that she may say no, it takes courage for a boy to ask a girl for a date. It may involve major inner emotional struggles. Thus, girls asking would help some worthy, bashful boys to get into the courtship processes.

Mary, who has dated John a few times, is usually labeled as "going steady," and boys thus by-pass her. If she ceases dating John, under the system of equality, she could ask Robert for a date, and thus quickly get back into the stream of courtship prospects.

There is a shortage of boys in some areas and some communities. Under equality, girls would be given an equal opportunity in the courtship processes.

The courtship role is a major, crucial, and decisive part of planning life's future. Nature and society have thrust upon women the responsibility of childrearing. She is thus forced to give up, for a time, a career outside the home and much social interaction. We have observed that mature, secure, young women do not object to the career of motherhood. Surely, society owes it to them to give them the right to choose a companion to walk by their side—one who would be meaningful to them especially during their years of childbearing and child rearing.

Under the doctrine of equality, both boys and girls would take the initiative in courtship. Their courtship would be a joint planning process in which both understand each other and themselves as fully as possible. Under submissive courtship, marriage for the bride is often a leap in the dark instead of a wise step forward. Equality would in no way change their roles in marriage. Each would still be responsible for the necessary roles the Creator-God planned for them.

Personality Development

The doctrine of husband and wife equality should help to develop well-balanced personalities in both husband and wife. It should promote and organize behavioral and emotional tendencies in line with biblical values, attitudes, and motives. The personality characteristics of both husband and wife should rise above hostility, envy, jealousy, and other offensive habits.

They will live together in harmony and in love as though they had only one mind and one spirit between them. They will not act from motives of rivalry or personal vanity, but in humility think more of one another than they do of themselves. They will not think only of their own affairs, but each will learn to see things from the other's point of view.[5]

Self-esteem

Equality should lead husband and wife to meet each other's emotional needs and accomplish each other's personal fulfillment. All human beings have built-in needs for self-confidence and self-esteem. The hierarchy teaching tends to cause the husband to think of himself more highly than he should and tends to undermine the self-esteem of the wife.

Protection Against an Insecure Husband

Equality should protect a wife from being dominated by an insecure husband. Insecurity is one of the major emotional problems of all people, both men and women. There are lots of insecure husbands. Insecure people through lack of self-confidence tend to be ruled by fear. They become very sensitive, very jealous, and are easily offended. They carry chips on their shoulders. They tend to be very critical of others and often punish people for doing well what they themselves are afraid to do. Overt aggressiveness is used to suppress other people and thereby their inner security is masked. In this situation, an insecure husband has a psychological club he can use on his subservient wife, and she is left largely defenseless. Under the equality doctrine both husband and wife have psychological protection against any insecurities which may exist in their spouse. Equality in Christ is the surest way to guarantee equality and justice for all. With excellent insight on this subject James H. Olthuis aptly remarks:

> Although at times it may seem easier to let one partner take over, a husband and wife can jeopardize their entire relation by establishing a male-dominated marriage. When a woman virtually surrenders her personality to her husband, she has less to give to the relationship as the years pass. Outwardly she may seem rather content, but inwardly she grows more and more dependent until she is only an adjunct. Often powerful feelings of hostility well up inside her, against herself for succumbing and against her husband (and God) for demanding such subservience. She feels her marriage is a "trap" with four walls and a husband as keeper.
>
> The situation becomes more complicated when the husband continues to grow through outside contacts while the wife languishes at home. He may have begun to grow away from her when he promised to keep his office problems out of the home. Unfortunately, after years of living separate lives, he may begin to feel that his wife no longer has the understanding to be his confidante and equal. Despite her

dutiful obedience and continual adoration, he begins to see her as an embarrassment. Sometimes, feeling guilty, he pampers her even more (just the wrong thing if he wants her to grow up); at other times he suddenly drops her for "no apparent reason," using her childish behavior (accentuated by his pampering) to justify an affair.[6]

Communication

The equality concept tends to promote communication between husband and wife. Communication is a part of the cement that holds both the foundation and the superstructure of a marriage together. Without communication, a marriage drifts into a twilight zone of coexistence. Although the hierarchy defenders deny it, the submissive teachings often tend to make the husband-wife communication a one-way street. Guidelines tend to flow from the husband to the wife, and she is supposed to follow. Under equality the attitudes and understanding between husband and wife are so structured that each listens actively to the other, and each responds in warm language. It is a two-way street. Questions and answers are welcome. They can, in complete trust, each let down their external defenses and bare their inner feelings and arrive at patterns of understanding between them that are Christian and that are best for both.

Strong Personalities

Husband-wife equality provides a healthy family environment for growing children, that is, a mother and father in a happy love relationship. Life should be easier when children grow up in an atmosphere of male-female equality. If husband and wife follow equality patterns of behavior, it should tend to develop strong personal ties with relatives, in-laws, neighbors, and the community at large.

Community Benefits

An active doctrine of equality tends to give balance, wholeness, and unity to marriage. It should release much energy for husband and wife to be utilized in absorbing creative projects outside of themselves, involving others in the home and community. It should develop a spiritual, moral, and social fiber of the home and community that would decrease extramarital sex relations, broken families, and divorces. A community with a healthy family life should be able to develop an effective social structure.

God's Plan

Finally, the doctrine of equality should tend to develop a close, warm, personal, and spiritual relationship between husband and wife and God. The equality doctrine, if taken seriously, and followed faithfully day after day, should place any husband and wife on the cutting edge and the growing edge of life's realities as planned by God our Creator.

With this we rest our case. We now turn our attention to the process of applying the biblical doctrine of husband-wife equality to practical everyday experiences in both their domestic relationships and their one-flesh sexual relationships.

PART II

DOMESTIC EQUALITY

4

Under Equality How Does a Couple Decide Who Does What?

Under a system of husband-wife equality, what roles should each spouse play in the home and community? The term *role* refers to what society expects of husband and wife and what husband and wife expect of each other. We need to distinguish between two facts: (1) In God's plan for marriage, husbands and wives are equal, and neither is superior nor inferior. (2) Because of the basic biological differences inherent in male and female, they need to perform different roles in the home and community. This in no way weakens, reduces, or nullifies their equality.

When a young couple gets married with opposite views of husband-wife roles, there is always trouble ahead! For example, let us imagine the following situation: David Bell, twenty years old, lived on Avenue A, in Middletown, USA. He is a mature and responsible young man. His mother has never worked outside of the home for pay. She has always been a homemaker. She kept David's clothing mended and his shirts washed and ironed. She cooked the food David liked, and the cookie jar was kept filled. David loved his

mother. She loved him. They had a good mother-son relationship under these conditions. What was David's concept
of an ideal wife and mother? His mother!

One block away on Avenue B in Middletown there lived a
twenty-year-old woman, Janet Moore. She is a mature and
responsible young woman. Her mother has always been a
schoolteacher. Janet cannot remember when her mother
was not teaching school. As a result Janet had to learn to do
many things in the home such as cooking, sewing, and
housecleaning. Janet loved her mother. Her mother loved
Janet. It was a good mother-daughter relationship under
these conditions. What was Janet's concept of an ideal wife
and mother? Her mother!

In due time David and Janet were attracted to each other
and went through the normal processes of courtship and
were married. Both sets of parents and the community were
happy because David and Janet were such fine young
people. Neither the Bells nor the Moores were wealthy
people, so David and Janet had to buy furniture on the
installment plan. Janet asked David if she could go to work
as a bank teller to help pay for the furniture. David did not
like the idea, but reluctantly agreed that she could work for
only one year, until they had paid for the furniture. After
the honeymoon David and Janet both worked from eight
until five with an hour off for lunch. When they got home
each day at 5:30, guess who got busy and cooked the evening meal? You know who! Guess who washed the dishes
after the evening meal? You know who! Guess who did the
washing and ironing each weekend? You know who! Guess
who cleaned and dusted the house each week? You know
who! In David's mind, housework was a woman's work.
Janet loved David. She knew how to do housework efficiently. So she pitched in and did all the housework on
evenings and weekends, while David read the paper,
watched TV, and read books. This meant that Janet had to
do two jobs. After some weeks Janet became nervous,

tense, and exhausted because of the situation—doing two full-time jobs. As a result, gradually David and Janet drifted into disagreement and quarreling. Their dream of a good marriage was fast falling apart. *Why?* Simply because they entered marriage with opposite ideas about husband-wife roles.

Under the doctrine of equality, how does a couple decide on husband-wife roles? In other words, who does what in housework, child care, and wage earning?

Elisabeth Elliot unfairly criticized the equality doctrine (as related to roles) by saying that under equality there are "power struggles" between husband and wife. There is petty childish "scorekeeping." Efforts are made to see that one does not outdo the other. She talks of binding marriage contracts in which each detail of who does what is spelled out. She pictures husband and wife keeping score and sitting down on Saturday to add up the score to see that each does his part. She pictures the husband cooking or caring for the children on Tuesday, Thursday, and Saturday, and the wife on Monday, Wednesday, and Friday. When the wife does more than the husband one week, she pictures the husband doing more next week to balance things up. In her description, she assumes husband and wife are competitors, self-centered, lazy, stingy, immature, and selfishly concerned exclusively with his or her own pleasure, advantage, and well-being.[7] Mrs. Elliot's description of husband-wife roles under equality is as far from reality as the East is from the West.

Who does what under equality would vary according to the particular situation at the time. For example, in an ideal family situation, roles played would gradually change across the years. They would vary in the following situations: (1) The couple is just married and both work at public jobs. (2) The wife is working while the husband is in college or graduate school. (3) The wife is working in the home and caring for small children. The husband is working outside the home. (4) The children are grown and gone, but the wife prefers not to work outside the home for pay. (5) The children are grown and gone, and the wife works outside of the home for pay.

In the process of living together as husband and wife, there are two major tasks—household responsibilities and financial support. Under Christian equality, each can be managed and directed to operate efficiently for the good of both husband and wife. Each calls for time, energy, and work. Each brings some happiness, growth, progress, and maturity to both marriage partners. The home must be a major priority in the life of both husband and wife, and the occupation must be a major priority in the life of both husband and wife.

Because of the nature of love and the constantly changing life situations, it would be irrational and ridiculous to list details of what every husband and wife should do under equality. What each does could vary from day to day, week to week, month to month, and year to year. Remember, our definition of husband-wife equality says that God established in Creation a husband-wife relationship in which freedom and independence are equal, dependence and trust are mutual, and responsibility and reliability are reciprocal. Husband and wife are in a parallel mutual relationship of unity and equality in which each behaves toward the other in love, in grace, in privilege, and in spiritual joy as a person of worth. They are equals in self-surrender and devotion to each other. They are both leaders. They are both followers. They are both authority. They are both submissive. They are both dominant. They are both subordinate. They are both protectors. They are both spiritual and physical partners in a "one-flesh" unity that is a two-way street. They are "subject to one another out of reverence for Christ."

5

Under Husband-Wife Equality: Who Makes the Final Decision?

It seems that the point at which the traditional thinkers have the greatest difficulty in accepting the theory of equality is how to break the impasse when husband and wife disagree, if one does not have the final authority.

There are several possible ways for a couple to make a decision when they disagree on some specific problem.

1. The husband could make the decision. But this is the traditional hierarchy system. It tends to neglect the rights and needs of the wife. Due to the self-centered nature of men, they would tend to take unfair advantage of their wives.
2. The wife could make the decision. This tends to neglect the rights and needs of the husband. Due to the self-centered nature of women, they would tend to take unfair advantage of their husbands.
3. A third possible solution would be for the husband and wife to take turns making decisions. This tends to develop competition between husband and wife. It advocates a kind of 50–50 equality which just does not work. It sounds more like the behavior of little children than mature adults.
4. A fourth possible solution is to enter into a debate and openly argue the question until one side wins. This sets up personal conflict between husband and wife. Argu-

ment is the crutch of lame minds. The situation becomes emotional. Glands pour adrenalin into the bloodstream, and both prepare for battle. Each will be determined to win the argument. Each may use small part-truths or ideas not based upon fact in order to get his way. This emotional type of conflict can turn into a struggle in which they physically slug it out. Mature persons do not accept verbal and physical force as an adult way of settling differences between people.

5. A fifth possible solution would be to agree on a compromise halfway between each other's wants or desires. However, the final decision may not be the one that best meets their needs.

6. Let us assume that husband and wife have agape love for each other and that both are mature Christians. Under these circumstances both would want to seek divine leadership in the matter. They would pray individually and together for God's leadership. They would freely and objectively discuss all sides of the problem. In this humble, contrite attitude, sensitive to God's will and the needs and rights of one another, they will usually both come to a decision that is acceptable to both and that meets the rights and needs of both. The final decision may be completely different from what either had proposed, or it may follow the idea of one spouse more than the other. Regardless of the final nature of the decision, both would recognize that the decision was best for the rights and needs of both and was, to the best of their ability, the will of God. (Notice that in this process of decision making the freedom and identity of each individual are preserved, and unity and equality are both maintained.)

At the same time we must be realistic and call attention to the fact that men and women tend to view life experiences differently and that any two people, regardless of sex, at times are certain to disagree, because of differences in life experiences, life motivations, and life goals. But disagreement need not be cause for alarm. In fact, in husband-wife equality where each feels free to express his or her views, there will be less emotional impact because, as Christians, each learns to respect the opinions of the other, and thus less harm is done to the marriage relationship.

What is it that causes husband and wife to get into struggle and conflict over decision making? It is largely just plain old-fashioned selfishness, self-centeredness, insecurity, immaturity, and sinfulness. What is it that enables husband and wife to make joint decisions without struggle and conflict? It is just plain New Testament Christianity in which both want to follow the will of God in Christian love and both are sensitive to—and more concerned about—meeting the rights and needs of the other than of self.

It has been said that there are three sides to everything: your side, my side, and the right side. We might state it better by saying your side, my side, and the side that is in accord with truth, Christian love, and the purpose and will of God!

If we say that when husband and wife cannot agree on a decision, the husband should make the decision, this changes things. The husband becomes the final authority, the wife becomes subordinate and many interpersonal problems may enter their marriage relationships that tend to undermine, erode, and destroy their unity, equality, and their individual and marriage happiness.

To allow either husband or wife to have the authority to make the final decisions is bad thinking. The words of a children's verse are pertinent.

Bad thought is a thief,
He plays a part,
Sneaks in through the windows of our hearts.
And if, once, his way he wins,
He lets a hundred robbers in.

The concept of husband (or wife) having the authority to make final decisions is a bad thought. Once it is accepted, there will automatically follow a tangled web of harmful and injurious concepts which will tend to block husband-wife mutuality, happiness, and fulfillment. Let us repeat: a committee of two has no chairman.

6

Should Wives Work Outside the Home for Pay?

In rural America from 1776 to World War II, the role of the wife was in the home, and the husband's role was to take full responsibility for the financial support of the family. It was assumed that any variation from that norm would threaten the stability of the home. Our society moved away from that norm when women were asked to take secular employment and replace men, who were then in the armed forces, in order to win World War II. Since then, there has been (1) an increasing number of women receiving higher education; (2) an increased emphasis on the rights of individuals; and (3) many conservative Christian thinkers who are saying that the Bible really teaches husband-wife equality. These and other social movements have increased the number of wives working outside the home for pay. This presents major social problems.

There is no easy answer to the question, "Should women work outside of the home for pay?" Each family must be considered separately according to its own peculiar situation. It should be decided on the basis of the needs and rights of the husband, the wife, their marriage, and their children. What is the purpose and will of God in these areas? In Bible times life was rural, and most wives were homemakers. Yet some of the leading women of the Bible worked to help support the family. Who? Lydia (Acts 16:14,

15); Priscilla (Acts 18:2, 3; 24–26); and the woman described in Proverbs 31:10–31.

There are two sides to this problem. Let us objectively examine both sides. In the following home situations it would be questionable for a wife to work outside the home in regular employment:

No Situations

1. Homes with preschool children. Preschool years are the most impressionable years. A child can never make up for the loss of learning and training in a good home during his formative preschool years. During these years the emotional stability, moral values of right and wrong, and personality traits are determined. Being left at a day nursery or with a baby-sitter may cause a child to feel rejected and leave permanent emotional scars.
2. Homes where the wife finds complete fulfillment in the role of homemaker, and her spiritual, intellectual, social, and emotional needs are met through church and community contacts. The idea that a woman can find complete personal fulfillment *only* in a professional career is a deadly myth.
3. Homes where a working wife means that the husband's and wife's time together is limited to the point where communication is minus zero.
4. Homes where the motivation for a working wife is simply to have access to more money for pride and social power in order to "keep up with the Joneses."
5. Homes where the husband is very insecure and whose ego would be threatened if his wife had to work to supplement the family income.
6. Homes where the wife feels unloved by her husband and seeks the contacts of outside employment to build up her ego and her sense of self-worth. This is often the path to an affair, a broken home, and the divorce court.

Yes Situations

Now, we need to study the flip side of this problem. The following family situations indicate that a wife's employment outside the home could be the better part of wisdom:

1. Homes where a widowed wife with children must work to pay for food, clothing, rent, and other necessities of life.
2. Homes where the husband has been laid off from his work and job opportunities in his field of experience are scarce. Often a wife can secure employment and help maintain a decent standard of living until he can be re-employed. Meanwhile he assumes most of the responsibilities of the children and the home.
3. Homes where the husband's health does not permit employment necessary to support the family, but he is able and willing to assume some or most of the responsibility of the children and the home.
4. Homes where the children are in college and the wife must secure employment in order to assure the children a college education.
5. Homes where there are no children (either they've never had any, or their children are grown and gone) and the wife feels the need to utilize her skills and talents in a vocation which helps her to grow as a person, and will make a contribution to society.

When a family situation justifies wife employment and both husband and wife are still living, they must carefully follow standards that are both intelligent and Christian in order to avoid conflict and to enjoy marriage happiness. The following guidelines should be helpful:

Guidelines for Working Couples

1. The will of God for individuals including husband, wife and each child should take precedence over cultural trends. Cultural trends are largely dictated by vested

interests and social climbers. They drift and meander aimlessly to and fro in derelict fashion, all the while ignoring human values, rights, and needs.

2. The personal attitudes and feelings of the husband or wife toward the wife's being gainfully employed must be considered. To force a life pattern on one's companion against his or her will can undermine and destroy a marriage.

3. During wife employment, husband and wife (and children, if any) must work out a plan for equally sharing in household tasks, so that the wife is not overburdened by trying to do two jobs—the home responsibilities *and* outside employment. When both husband and wife work outside the home for pay, they are both equally responsible for performing the household chores.

4. Either the husband or the wife should be at home when the children come home from school and should be in their life experience the rest of the day, not as a dictator, but as a loving, concerned parent and leader.

5. All family income, whether earned by husband or wife or both, belongs to both and should be administered through a joint checking account.

6. There must be a careful budgeting of time so that often, at least once a week, there can be a block of time for family activities.

7. Last, but certainly not least, both husband and wife need to budget time daily so they can talk, plan, and share their lives and their love with each other. The lack of shared time alone between husband and wife, where tender loving communication flows freely, is a major cause for unhappiness in marriage. Christian agape love calls for husband-wife equality, and both call for participation in mutual sharing of self to one another.

7

Helpful Habits for Husbands and Wives

In a marriage relationship of equality, what conduct and patterns of behavior does a man look for in his wife, and what conduct and patterns of behavior does a woman look for in her husband? The concern here is not roles, as such, but rather the concern is the everyday idiosyncrasies, interpersonal habits, and specific behavior characteristics between husband and wife that each likes and dislikes about the other.

Helpful Habits for Husbands

During courtship a man puts his "best foot" forward in order to win his sweetheart, and rightly so. He is concerned about being well groomed and neat in appearance. A man needs to continue this pattern in marriage. If he is an automobile mechanic, or if he works in a coal mine, or a glue factory, his wife will not expect him to come home looking and smelling like a rose. She will understand when he comes home greasy, dirty, and smelly. And she will not expect him to wear a tuxedo around the house. But a man can avoid the look and smell of a "nasty, unclean beast." A wife enjoys seeing her husband reasonably neat and clean around the house.

During courtship a man puts his sweetheart on a pedestal and worships her as a goddess. In marriage, he must not go to the other extreme and make her a slave by putting her "neck under his foot." Rather, in marriage husbands and wives are equals! Partners! Neither is inferior or superior! They complement and supplement each other! A man should always respect his wife as his equal!

A husband ought to be gentle and courteous to his wife. He should always show her respect and common politeness and be mindful of her rights and her needs. Some husbands come home tired and impatient but never give their wives the right to be tired and impatient.

A man must be fair in all financial matters. All of the money that both husband and wife have belongs to both of them. As equal partners, both should decide how, when, and where their money will be used. (*See* chapter 8.)

A man ought to be sociable at home with his wife and his children. Some husbands are exceedingly entertaining at work or out in company—the life of the party. At home they close up like a bank vault at night. This is difficult for wives to understand. Wives like fun, laughter, and companionship at home with their husbands. Certainly there are occasions when shared tears build strong ties, but we suggest that often-shared laughter between husband and wife builds even stronger ties.

A husband needs to show his wife kindness, tenderness, and appreciation. She enjoys hearing her husband say, "I love you." Too many husbands are like the man in this story: The husband had been sick, bedfast for twenty years. His wife had cared for him "hand and foot" during all that time. During those years he had never once told her that he loved her. One day she got the courage to ask him why. He replied, "Now, Matilda, when I married you, I told you that I loved you. If I change my mind, I'll let you know." Although this story usually brings some laughter, we have a feeling it won't be very funny to far too many wives.

Wives appreciate small attentions and thoughtfulness from their husbands. A wife wants her husband to be aware of her and her interests. She appreciates a telephone call when he is delayed in keeping an appointment with her. Suppose a husband promises to meet his wife at 12:00 noon to take her to lunch. At ten o'clock an emergency arises, and it is obvious that he will be delayed one hour. Suppose he telephones his wife and says, "Sweetheart, I am going to be delayed one hour and I wanted you to know." She will wait an hour and be happy as a lark. Why? *He thought about me! "I wanted you to know."* If he does not call his wife and stands her up for one hour, he has willfully violated the person he ought to love best.

A wife appreciates compliments on her new dress, hairdo, and the good meal she cooked. She wants to feel that she is loved. She wants her friends to know that he loves her. She wants to feel needed and that her opinions are valued. To be assured that she is somebody is a melody that she never grows tired of. If he finds fault with her, she will be hard to live with. If he tells her that she is wonderful, she will break her neck to be a perfect wife. Show us a woman who is crazy about "things," who lives to keep up with the Joneses, and we'll show you a woman who doesn't feel loved by her husband. Of course, the desire for love, kindness, and appreciation can be carried to neurotic extremes. The need for love and appreciation is a two-way street. If a husband shows his wife tenderness, love, and appreciation he will never have the problem of her refusing to meet his sexual needs. And he will not be bothered with the problem of a frigid wife.

It is so easy for a husband to take advantage of his wife because of his occupational responsibilities, the nature of the social and economic community organization, and the nature of the human male (physical strength and strong sex drive). A husband must be constantly on guard, alert; he must use ingenuity and positive action or he will slip into the rut of mistreating his wife, the bride of his youth. It is not where you are on the road that is important. The direction in which you are headed is the important thing.

Helpful Habits for Wives

A husband wants his wife to be alive, to have enthusiasm and gaiety, yet not be boisterous. He wants his wife to have a sense of humor, especially the ability to laugh at herself. He wants a wife who can soothe hectic situations, rather than stirring them up by "throwing gasoline on the fire." He wants a wife who will not peddle stories about the home and the business that would be better left unsaid. He wants a wife with high values and ideals, one who is feminine, modest, happy, who smiles, and laughs. He enjoys her when she is jolly, vivacious, and frolicsome; yet he wants her to possess dignity.

Most husbands like their wives to be natural rather than artificial. They dislike the siren or Hollywood type of woman. They detest the woman who goes to excess in the use of make-up—long barn-red fingernails, haystack hairdos, two black eyes, and lipstick one-eighth inch thick. It doesn't taste good. This doesn't mean that men completely reject all feminine make-up—not at all.

Husbands dislike wives who are catty, critical, and nagging. They hate to come home each evening to complaints and tales of woe. They do not want their wives to save up whipping of the children until "their father comes home." Some wives start by saying, "First, I want you to whip Johnny for this, and Susie for that, and Billy for this." Obviously this is not a pleasant homecoming for a husband. Most husbands understand that there are many problems related to the children and the home during the day and week that need and must have their attention and help. When possible, it is better for the wife not to begin on him as soon as he arrives home, but wait a little while, maybe later in the evening or the weekend when there is more relaxed time.

We are reminded of a story told by Dr. L. R. Scarborough many years ago. It seems that the hired cook came in the back door to start plans for getting breakfast at 5:00

A.M. She was frightened by a snake that had managed to crawl into the kitchen. She rushed to the master bedroom, knocked, and demanded that Dr. Scarborough get up and kill the snake. He said, "Go upstairs and wake up our son and tell him to kill the snake." She followed orders, but the son said, "You kill it; it is too early for me to get up." As the cook went back downstairs, she was overheard to say, "What we need is a 'man-person' around this house." Most husbands realize that their wives want and need their masculine help about domestic problems. A little planning, dialogue, understanding, and systematic organization ought to handle this need to the satisfaction of both wife and husband.

A man does not like to become involved in conflict and emotional discussion with his wife. Constant annoyance, fretting, and nagging may drive him from the home.

Sometimes a husband's greatest need is something as simple as sex. Husbands often complain that their wives are too tired, too busy, or too cold to be able to meet their needs. Many wives simply do not understand the urgency of the sex drive of their husbands. Let us hasten to say that this is neither malicious nor willful on the part of a wife. It is rooted in the fact that she is a woman and not a man, and that she misjudges his feelings and needs. A wife should understand that her husband's self-confidence is directly related to the success of his sexual life. She must also understand the need to accept the fact that the strong sexual desire of her husband manifests itself somewhat differently from her own sexual nature. A wife needs to know that her husband feels he is a worthless heel, when his wife does not enjoy sex life with him. Contrary to what some women think, most husbands do not want sex without love from them. (The problem of sexual adjustment in marriage will be discussed in Part III.)

8

Who Should Hold the Purse Strings?

Charles Cooper was a successful lawyer in a small southern city of about ten thousand population. In addition to his profession, he was a real estate agent and owned much property; he handled all business and financial matters. He gave Karen a small sum each month to use for groceries, clothing, and other family expenses. The amount was too small to care adequately for the family needs. Karen planned and skimped and managed to get by, but food was less than adequate, clothing was shabby, and the furniture was worn with wear and tear of many winters. Karen had learned through bitter experience not to ask for more money to run the home. Charles was now director in the local bank and was one of the more wealthy men in the county. He was the authority over the money of the family and ruled with an iron hand. Money and real estate were first in his life. He acted and planned as if he would live forever. At age fifty-five Charles dropped dead of a heart attack. Then Karen had the responsibility of taking over his financial empire. She knew nothing about the details of his financial situation. Two months after Charles's death, Karen found that she owned some property she did not know they had.

Although Charles was not well acquainted with the doctrine of family hierarchy, he was certainly practicing it. Let me hasten to say that we cannot hold current hierarchy thinkers responsible for the many "Charles Coopers" in our society. However, the problem of the husband-wife finances does furnish an excellent area where husband and wife equality can be efficiently and visibly put into practice for the good of all concerned.

Economic Partners

Research shows that money conflict is probably the second largest problem in marriage. There are no bosses in happy families. Under the Christian teaching of equality, husband and wife are partners in marriage, not competitors; sweethearts, not enemies; friends not foes. Who should control the purse strings? Both! Both partners! Both the husband and the wife!

There *is* scientific evidence that the husband and wife are really equal economic partners. Suppose a wife works out of the home for pay two years before her children are born. During this period all of the money that both of them make belongs to both of them. When their children are born, the wife works in the home, without pay. Yet all of the money that the husband makes belongs to both of them. Suppose that after two children are born, the wife should die? What would it cost the husband to hire help to do all of the work that she was doing, at the then-prevailing wage? Several family scholars have made careful studies of this, and the results show that it would cost him as much money as his salary, and some studies have shown that it would cost more. Since the mother of children, on the average, is really earning as much money (but getting no pay) as the father is, all of the money that he makes belongs to both of them, and they should both decide together on how to use it. In the past, this fact has often been overlooked, and some husbands, like Charles Cooper, have kept their wives in financial prison by doling out miserly small amounts for them to buy food, to purchase clothing, and to run the home. Some husbands add insult to injury by nagging their wives for being spendthrifts. Such selfish behavior can only cause frustration and conflict between the husband and wife.

When all the children are grown and married, the wife may again work outside the home for pay. The equality principle still prevails; all the money that both make belongs to both of them, and they decide together as partners how the money will be used.

Expenditure Discussions

Since they are partners, both have a right to have some money in their purse at all times to spend for small items that men and women need. They should discuss in conference general guidelines to be followed when large sums of money are involved. They should discuss it and agree before the money is spent. A husband does not have a moral right to trade their old car in for an expensive new one without discussing it with his wife. A wife does not have a moral right to purchase expensive new living-room furniture without discussing it with her husband. They are equal partners and should behave as equal partners. But in marriage, personal love for each other demands (even more than the concept of economic partners) that husband and wife respect each other's rights and wishes as related to money. Love is not a selfish, stingy skinflint. Love is flexible! Love respects! Love trusts!

When husband and wife are both working and the monthly or weekly payday arrives, they should first set aside at least one-tenth for Christian service through their church. Then they should take out a mutually agreed amount to put into their savings account. Next they should take out a given amount of cash. The wife should put half of it in her purse and the husband should put the other half in his purse. The remainder of their combined checks should be deposited in the bank in a joint checking account. When the husband runs out of cash first, his wife should divide half of what she has left with him, and vice versa. When both are out of pocket cash, they should write a check for cash and divide it equally between them and so on. Thus both will always have access to some money in their purses. Both write checks according to their agreed guidelines. It is not important who writes the check or pays for the groceries or the gasoline. The important thing is that a couple have an economic plan as partners, and respect each other's rights and needs.

These suggestions assume that both husband and wife have healthy attitudes toward life. It assumes that they would follow such guidelines as: Neither the husband or wife is superior or inferior. Both are superior to animals and things. Money is not an end in itself; it is a tool to be used. Money should not be worshipped, nor should it be abused.

If either husband or wife turns out to be an extreme spendthrift or a miser, the other must try slowly and skillfully to guide their economic plans away from those extremes toward efficiency and stability.

9

In-Law Relationships

If the doctrine of equality is accepted by the bride and groom as they move into marriage, it should promote good in-law relationships. It should cause them to have respect for both sets of in-laws, and to behave impartially toward them. If they accept each other as Christian equals, they would tend to think of each other's relatives as equals. However, the wife-subordinate teachings may cause some major problems among in-laws. This could easily be true of a husband's attitudes toward his wife's parents, if her parents are of a different social level from his parents.

Typical Example

Wade Clark was having major conflict with the parents of his wife, and Brenda, his wife, was having major conflict with Wade's parents. Wade's parents were well educated, socially sophisticated, and financially independent. Brenda's parents had only a high-school education and had to work hard to meet their financial needs. Wade would not visit her parents except in emergencies, and Brenda did not like to visit his parents. But Wade, being the head of the house, forced Brenda to visit his parents with him several times a year. During each visit Brenda was uptight, and her nerves were tied in knots. A fuss usually followed each visit, and it would take several days before they could get back to normal at home. Wade and Brenda loved each other, but were locked into a seemingly impossible in-law situation.

"Natural Conflict"

Some sociologists refer to the in-law relationships as being a "natural conflict" situation. A child lives twenty to twenty-two years with parents. A strong "we-group" is developed over the years. Parents love their children, and the children love their parents. This relationship becomes deep, intense, and personal, and rightly so. This close, intimate parent-child relationship that has developed for over twenty years does not disappear with the formality of a wedding ceremony. The parents of both the bride and the groom make suggestions after the marriage, and both bride and groom listen to their own parents. Each may accuse the other of allowing his parents to run them when both are doing the same thing. Thus, in-law relationships seem to be a natural conflict situation.

The In-Law Stereotype

Also, a joking, laughing attitude about in-laws in our society has stereotyped in-law problems as being greater than they really are. (The word *stereotype* is a sociological term that comes from the printing office. A metal plate is cast and placed in a printing machine, and every time the plate moves down to touch the paper, it prints the same thing.) Thus in society we form mental images about certain people, and every time that person is mentioned, we react to the preconceived mental image, instead of the reality. To name a few, we have stereotyped Scotsmen, Jews, Indians, blacks, and in-laws, especially mothers-in-law.

The stereotypes often take the form of jokes. For example, "The only difference between in-laws and out-laws is that the in-laws promise to pay it back." Or, there is the story illustrating the word *ambivalence* (having opposite emotions at the same time, such as happiness and sadness). "Mary was ambivalent when her mother-in-law drove their new Buick over a two-hundred-foot cliff. (It is sad to lose a new automobile.)"

A man took his dog to the vet to have his tail cut off. The vet said, "Sir, his tail has already been cut off once." "Yes, I know," he said, "but I want you to cut it off so short that there will be no tail left at all." "Okay," said the vet, "but I am curious as to why you want it so short." "Well," he said, "it is like this. You see, my mother-in-law is coming to visit in a month, and I don't want the slightest semblance of a welcome."

A cave man was busy in his cave beating out a stone ax. His wife came running into the cave shouting, "Husband come quick! A saber-tooth tiger is after mother." The husband kept on beating on his stone ax and said calmly, "What do you think I care what happens to that saber-toothed tiger?" We should note that these jokes, which may be funny, carry false stereotypes. Most mothers-in-law are fine people.

Possible Causes for Conflict

Sociological research indicates that approximately 77 percent of wives and 84 percent of husbands do not experience in-law problems. Thus, most couples get along well with their in-laws. Some studies show that the earlier the marriage age, the more in-law friction. This is because parents feel that their teenagers who have married are not yet mature enough to make right decisions in their marriage, so both sets of parents try to take over and run the marriage. The teenagers listen to their own parents and both call it in-law interference.

Other studies indicate that in-law conflict is a feminine habit more than a masculine habit. Mothers seem to be threatened more by daughters-in-law than sons-in-law. Women are involved in in-law friction six times more often than men, and mothers-in-law conflict problems are almost equal to all other in-law conflict combined. The structure of organized family life helps to explain this. The mother is with her child more than the father. Mother and children develop a close "we" relationship. Thus, her emotional ties to her children cause her to indicate greater interest in their marriage. Some studies show that in-law conflict is the greatest cause for separation or divorce during the first year of marriage. Obviously, conflict is less a problem for couples who have been married ten or twenty years.

Also, in-law friction tends to increase in mixed marriages, such as when a rural boy marries a city girl, a rich girl marries a poor boy, or a Catholic marries a Protestant. The more mixed the marriage, the higher the amount of in-law problems.

Thus, we conclude that in-law conflict is a largely feminine pattern, an early marriage problem, a mixed marriage problem.

How to Avoid In-Law Conflicts

What can husband and wife do to avoid in-law problems? A study of the Scriptures on in-law relations is in order. The Bible instructs that "a man should *leave* his father and mother and *cleave* to his wife . . ." (*see* Genesis 2:24). It also says to every person, "Honor your father and your mother . . ." (Exodus 20:12).

Generally both husband and wife feel the need of backing, support, love, and respect from their spouse in the presence of in-laws. When a husband visits his parents or her parents with his wife, he should be proud of her, give her compliments and let it be known that she is a wonderful wife. If he does so, his parents will be proud of him. Her parents will appreciate him. His wife will love him for it. Likewise, when a wife visits her parents or her husband's parents with her husband, she should be proud of him, give him compliments, and let it be known that he is a wonderful husband. If she does so her parents will be proud of her. His parents will appreciate her. Her husband will love her for it. Following this type of Christian equality can either solve in-law conflicts or keep them from developing into an open sore that may take years to heal.

10

Husband-Wife Religion

Pauline was an attractive high-school graduate who had worked five years in a local business. She was an active, committed Christian and had high moral standards. There were very few young men in her community who were marriage prospects. She had been dating Russell occasionally, but he was not a Christian and was lacking in positive moral characteristics. He was a weekend drinker and gambler. He was lazy, shiftless, and usually jobless. He begged Pauline to marry him. She talked to him about her church and what their religious life would be like after marriage. He solemnly promised her that if she would marry him he would "join her church." Finally, Pauline married Russell. After marriage, Russell kept putting off his promise. He not only failed to become a member of her church or any other church, but continued his questionable behavior to the embarrassment of Pauline and the community.

Definition of Terms

We need to distinguish between the terms *religion* and *Christianity*. Religion is an all-inclusive term that includes all people who worship and serve some kind of god or assumed supernatural power. Christianity is usually classified as a religion by many secular writers. We understand this to be a part truth in the sense that we worship and serve Jehovah God. However, the term religion includes many systems where people are worshiping finite gods they made with their own hands, gods that are powerless to help the worshipers. Christianity is a personal relationship with Jehovah God. In the best sense of the term, Christianity is not a religion. It is the worship and service of the infinite, omnipotent, eternal Jehovah God who revealed Himself to us in Jesus Christ who abides within us, and directs our lives through the Holy Spirit. Since Jehovah God is the only true God, Judeo-Christianity stands alone as the only system of faith and belief that works. All other religious systems are hopelessly searching for some impersonal god to help them.

How to Be Born Again

Also, we need to distinguish between "joining a church" and the process of a person being "born again." "Joining a church" is what happens when a person is received by a group of other persons who are organized as a church. It involves only human authority. It is simply an interpersonal human relationship of a person to a group of persons including the formalities and regulations of the group. The process of being "born again" is a relationship and a personal experience between a person and Jehovah God who has revealed Himself through His Son Jesus Christ, who was born of a virgin, crucified on the cross to atone for man's sin and who has risen from the dead; who ascended back to the Father, and who will come again to receive His own into eternal life.

What is man's part in his own salvation? In order to be born again a person (1) must believe that he is a sinner having sinned against God (Romans 3:23, 6:23); (2) must hear the Gospel (Romans 10:14); (3) must believe that he is lost (John 3:18, 36); (4) must repent of his sins (Luke 13:3; Acts 3:19, 17:30); and (5) must receive Jesus Christ as his personal Savior (John 1:12; Ephesians 2:8, 9; Revelation 3:20). At this point the repenting, believing sinner is born again. He is now a new person in Christ. This is a divine work of God's grace.

Why Marry a Christian?

The doctrine of equality of husband and wife fits hand and glove into the teachings God has revealed in Christ in the Scriptures. It rests upon the infinite worth of persons in God's plan. The committed Christian is bound to a set of Christian values. The Bible warns against Christians marrying non-Christians in order to help us make right marriage choices. Sociological research indicates that there are three times as many marriage failures among non-Christians as there are among Christians. Studies of non-Christian people show a much higher rate of divorce and marriage unhappiness than among Christians. Also, studies show that Christian marriages have a better sex life than non-Christian marriages.

The reasons for these differences are obvious. Christianity insists on respect for the rights of all persons. In society, a Christian tries to understand the viewpoint of other people. In a Christian marriage both husband and wife try to understand each other's habits, life experiences, values, and Christian beliefs. They build up one another's self-esteem. The indwelling Christ helps people to distinguish between right and wrong. Such a relationship with Christ causes them to follow certain right patterns of behavior and to avoid certain wrong patterns of behavior. Our Christian values help us to promote self-control. This means less conflict and quarreling in marriage.

Christianity is the key to the total personality and behavior of persons. The value system of non-Christians is the key to their total personality and behavior patterns. Christianity gives husband and wife an anchor in times of defeat, seeming failure, grievous misfortune, and disasters. It helps people to develop, sustain, and persevere in a balanced view of human existence and its problems. It helps them to come to grips with the realities of life, death, and eternity. When husband and wife are Christians they regard all persons as having worth, value, rights, and needs regardless of age, race, sex, personality, or social status. The indwelling Christ directs their attitudes and values in right directions. He causes them to love unlovable persons. He causes them to distinguish between persons and the behavior of persons. *A Christian assumes that all persons are equals—not in potentialities or achievements—but in worth, rights, and needs.*

When husband and wife are Christian, they not only look upon each other as equals, but they each put the other first and self second. This attitude is doubled and tripled in strength because of their love for one another. Thus it is no accident when Christian husbands and wives show up in scientific research as having a low rate of divorce and a high rate of happiness. The difference in Pauline and Russell's religious values cost Pauline a happy marriage. Pauline was committed to Christian values while Russell was committed to "irreligious" values. All people have a "religion" of some kind. No matter how irreligious a person may be, he does have a definite set of values which he follows as personal guidelines.

11

Married Love in the Empty Nest

Modern sociologists have used the term "empty nest" to refer to that part of the marriage cycle when a family's children are grown and the last one has married or left home, leaving the husband and wife alone at home. The term often implies that this leaves the home desolate and empty of anything and everything worthwhile. It implies incurable loneliness and certain decline. It implies a gradual mental, emotional, and physical sinking and wasting away, a period in which the approaching end is knocking at the door. These implications are *false*. They are—at best—a very small imaginary, negative part of reality. They are—at the worst—blind, subjective pessimism that overlooks 99 percent of reality. We know a couple who were both forty-five when their last child married. Many couples are only fifty or less.

Years of Promise

Regardless of age, *the nest is not empty*. Husband and wife are still in it. Most of them are happy, active, useful persons. They may have forty, forty-five or more years yet together. Instead of being an empty nest, the future years of that nest can be full and running over with growth, progress, creativity, maturity, security, plus personal and marital happiness, including spiritual, mental, emotional, social and sexual happiness. During these years, husband-wife equality may be more meaningful than ever. I hope some thoughtful reader will recommend a better name for the term *empty nest*—one that will fully describe the potential

74

of the future years of husband and wife after the children are all grown and gone.

How to Promote Married Love

What can husband and wife do to promote married love in their interpersonal relationships after the children are married, and now living in their own homes? They must have a plan and work the plan. The following suggestions should be helpful. They are the ideal and would have to be adjusted to fit varying home situations.

If possible, all meals should be eaten together. Meals should be a time of personal fellowship, communication, and planning. When expressing thanks at the table always hold hands, so that regardless of who leads the prayer, it will be symbolically a united prayer. Many people like a devotional reading of the Bible and prayer at breakfast. It is an excellent spiritual experience to give God some time in devotion and prayer at the beginning of the day when we are rested from a good night's sleep and our minds are refreshed, alert, and active. We prefer to have our daily devotionals in the morning at breakfast. We follow the devotional schedule in the *Home Life* magazine.[8] One of us reads the suggested Bible passage, and the other reads the devotional material for the day built on the Bible passage. Then with united hands the one who read the Bible leads in prayer. To be sure we share equally, we reverse the procedure on alternate days. Often we pause to comment on the Bible passage and devotional reading as related to life in general and to our lives. We find this a precious part of our day.

Obviously each couple would vary the nature of the devotional and prayer period and the time of day to fit their personal habits and needs. But we must not overlook that Married Love in the Empty Nest must have a daily period of Bible reading, devotion, and prayer. In religious devotionals, it is well to plan a weekly or monthly devotional prayer calendar to avoid shallow, empty routine and repetition.

From breakfast to the evening meal, each should spend the day in his or her own individual pursuits according to the occupation and the specific family situation, but at breakfast, each should share plans for the day. No newspaper at the breakfast table, please! You are mature partners, companions, and lovers, not thoughtless, self-centered babies.

When possible, husband and wife should shop together. It is an opportunity to enjoy personal companionship. (The smart shopper lists in advance things needed and avoids buying anything not on the list.)

Assuming that your life interests, like ours, tend toward mental activities, you must work hard to plan an efficient type of recreation and physical exercise *every day*. This should be enjoyed together, such as gardening, walking, jogging, swimming, bowling, golfing, or tennis.

Evenings Together

Husband and wife should spend the evenings at home together as often as possible. Couples who love each other enjoy sitting together talking, planning, sharing the day's experiences, reading aloud to each other, or occasionally watching a selected TV program. (We personally find that most TV programs are a miserable waste of time.) Your home should be a place where both the mind and the spirit grow together. Some evenings a couple should enjoy attending good programs of an aesthetic nature involving church activities, music, drama, and art. To avoid becoming self-centered, a couple should plan a goal of doing something at least once a week to bring happiness to someone else. This activity might involve calling someone who is lonely, taking some food to a shut-in, a hospital visit, inviting a small group in for a meal, or an evening of fellowship and games.

Express Your Love

If possible, couples should sleep in a double bed, and should have some time each night for physical contact in love expression for each other which would vary from simple snuggling to complete "one-flesh" fulfillment. Love should be unconditional. On awaking each morning, there should be tender communication and limited love expression as the new day dawns. The above plans should keep the channels of communication open and avoid conflicts and quarrels. Husband and wife should feel free to say to one another, "I think! I feel! I wish! I want! I'm afraid! I've been wondering about!"

Each person's individuality should be preserved with freedom of thought and ideas. Each should have some time alone away from the other, yet love and marriage wants and needs much time together. Two or more times a year a couple should get away from their daily routine and spend one or two days in the mountains or at the seashore to renew their marriage vows and refresh their love for each other. Some couples regularly celebrate their "mensiversary" (monthly anniversary date) by dining out.

Meet Total Needs

Couples should be health-conscious. Eat right, sleep eight hours a night, and keep weight down. As a goal for weight, use a health chart that gives normal weight according to height, body frame and age.

In your marriage, empty yourselves of yourselves, meet each other's total needs—spiritual, emotional, mental, sexual, social, and aesthetic. The husband should meet his wife's total needs. The wife should meet her husband's total needs. Thus both needs are met. This may be ideal, but this is the way love operates! This is the nature of love. What couple was it that said, "The empty nest is a sad, unhappy, and depressing time"? Whoever it was, the problem was due either to apathy, selfishness, laziness, or all three!

12

Communication: The Keystone to Husband-Wife Equality

Roy and Helen Bridges had been married eleven years, had four fine children, a stable occupation, a good income, and a nice home. Their marriage was happy the first few years. Lately they had been gradually drifting apart. The newspaper at breakfast, the television in the evening, and separate social functions took their toll. They seemed to be out of touch with each other. Conversation was formal and minimal. The warm glow of their early years had slipped away from them.

A Basic Cause for Conflict

Sociological research indicates that the major problems in marriage are often conflicts related to sex, money, in-laws, child training, religious beliefs, and social life. New findings indicate that lack of communication is one of the basic causes of all these conflicts. It is obvious that Roy and Helen's problem seems to be *lack of communication*. Sounds familiar? Unfortunately it does for thousands of couples.

In courtship, couples walk hand in hand, and talk and visit and laugh; during this process they explore each other's life and personality; gradually they develop rapport, empathy, sympathy, understanding, and love. This is communication! It is the cement that holds the foundation and the superstructure of both courtship and marriage together.

As in courtship, so in marriage; the warm glow of happiness involves continued talking, listening, walking, holding hands, laughing, and responding. It involves an equal exchange of ideas, thoughts, and feelings from husband to wife and from wife to husband. Real communication in marriage involves husband and wife equally exposing their inner selves, their feelings and attitudes, to each other on the same wavelength. This is equality in action. Roy and Helen seem to have drifted into a shadowy twilight zone of neglect, self-centeredness, laziness, unconcern, and disrespect. This is not marriage. This is coexistence. But it is not too late to remedy their problem. They need to turn back the clock of time literally, and rebuild their interpersonal love relationship with the cement of communication.

Drifting Apart

It is in order to ask how did they drift into this twilight zone of taking each other for granted? Why is it often difficult for marriage partners to communicate? In any marriage there will be some major differences in family background and training. These differences often result in marriages where a husband and wife, who love each other, have major personality differences, such as differences in emotional temperament and differences in values and moral judgments. During courtship, couples put their best foot forward to win each other, and the differences are avoided and not allowed to express themselves.

After marriage, when the newness of marriage wears off, these differences surface and their real selves are exposed to view for the first time. These differences may be loaded with many emotional feelings and attitudes that are in conflict with those of each spouse, and do not lend themselves to friendly conversation. Therefore, in order to avoid hurting each other, husband and wife often tend to communicate less and less about the realities of their inner feelings

and attitudes and a sort of "stand-offish" coexistence develops.

How to Regain the Glow

How can a couple regain the warm glow of their early
married life? They must each learn to listen actively. They
must not only listen, but they must actively respond to what
has been said in warm, empathetic, and intelligible language. They must show concern and respect for each
other's ideas even though they may disagree. Husband and
wife can love each other and disagree with one another
without being disagreeable. Christian love operates like
that. Husband and wife need to communicate about small
events and trifles in each other's activities and experiences.
When a couple is able to communicate about trifles, they
will be able to communicate about really important matters.
Couples should watch the tone of voice in responding to
each other. One's tone of voice may indicate displeasure
and anger, or it may indicate the warm glow of tender love.

Husband and wife should plan united activities that bring
them in close personal association. Being interested in the
same activities promotes communication. Joint religious activities, exercise, family outings, social life, and time alone
together would be helpful.

Thus the Roys and the Helens, in order to regain the
warm glow of their early marriage, must both develop, not a
50–50 but a 100 percent–100 percent love communication in
which they each are 100 percent concerned about meeting
the other's total needs on all levels, including the spiritual,
mental, emotional, sexual, and social. This is equality in
action.

13

Husband-Wife "Busyness"

Another fear that people who advocate the wife-submissive theory express is that if the principle of equality is practiced and the wife is encouraged to express her freedom for personal development, she is likely to become so involved in community activities that their home life is neglected. This can be true for the husband as well as the wife, however.

Outside Activities

In the modern American family, it is normal to hear: "Don't wait dinner for me tonight, dear, I'll be late getting away from the office." Or, "Sorry I have to run, dear, but I'm late for the club meeting. Your dinner is warming in the oven." *Busy! Busy! Busy!* Modern husbands and wives are overwhelmed by pressures to participate in social organizations, civic clubs, voters' leagues, bowling leagues, community drives, Scouts, and a multitude of other groups. Those who do not respond to every call are often branded as unsocial or unpatriotic. Many of these organized groups are led by persons inspired with noble aims. Each may feel his organization is necessary to save youth and stabilize the community. Of course, some community organization is good and necessary; but today's community pressure on family life often is organization "gone wild."

Planning Is the Answer

Four facts are clear. First, the importance of the family is inherent in the plan of the Creator. Second, much of the organized pressure on the family is motivated by selfish vested interests. Third, community social groups cannot meet the total needs of human personality. Finally, if modern families are to be saved from the destroying influences of these pressures, they must resist through creative planning.

What can families do? Christian husbands and wives must study and heed the teaching of the Scriptures concerning their laziness. Paul said to the Ephesians, "Make the best use of your time, despite all the evils of these days. Don't be vague but grasp firmly what you know to be the will of the Lord (Ephesians 5:16, 17 PHILLIPS). Also, he said to the Colossians, "Conduct yourselves wisely toward outsiders, making the most of the time" (Colossians 4:5).

The Danger Signals

A family must recognize the danger signals which indicate that its schedule is overloaded. These are some of the signals: A husband and wife become so busy with community affairs that they have little or no time together. Children, needing parental interest and understanding, receive only the tag end of the day. Members of the family seldom eat together. The atmosphere in the home is tense. Each member of the family is chiefly concerned with his own plans, needs, and rights. Laughter, fun, and play in the family are missing. Members of the family have little in common. As communication declines, they drift apart. Church loyalty is gradually undermined by other demands on the family.

Learn to Say *No*

What can be done when these danger signals appear? Husband and wife must first determine that they will do something about "family busyness." There is no magic that will solve the problem. The doctrine of husband-wife equality should be helpful. *Husband and wife must equally take the initiative*. They must have a determined iron will. They must learn the art of saying *no*. Outside activities must be limited. Family activities must be planned. A weekly family conference should be held at a time when all the family can be present. The family may discuss plans for the week or month, including the family budget, the needs of each member of the family, and plans for joint family activities. The husband and wife must make definite decisions about the family schedule and reduce busyness.

The Family Conference Decides

In this democratic family conference, all members of the family, including the children, are heard. As children are trained to help plan family activities, they will learn to assume greater responsibilities. This tends to develop in them a spirit of cooperation, courtesy, and unselfishness. Some basic principles might be adopted to guide the family conference. Age levels and interest should be weighed carefully. The family conference could plan such activities as family worship, the family meal, cook-outs, family shopping, camping, picnics, and other recreation.

In making decisions, the family conference should consider these questions: Does this activity help create maturity? Will it conflict with the needs of husband and wife or of the children? How much time would it require? Will it interfere with health, work, school responsibilities, or church loyalty? Will this activity lead to other activities which may be morally or spiritually dangerous?

A time should be set aside each week for family group activities. A list of possible activities would be helpful in planning ahead. A family bulletin board or calendar can be used as a reminder and an aid in planning.

Planning and Leadership

Wise planning produces a proper balance between group activities within the home and outside the home. Husbands and wives must recognize that family busyness can eat away the foundations of their homes and their spiritual life. Too often excess community organization openly competes with Christian and church activities. Some have said that the only social life some people have is in and through their church life. They speak as if such people seem to forget or ignore that Christian fellowship in church life and its activities are also social. Could it be that the purest form of social life is found in the modern churches of the community? Could it be that the best interests of personality growth and development are often violated by excess community organization?

Through strong, positive leadership on the part of both husband and wife as equals, they can protect their homes from excess community busyness. It is not altogether the amount of time that husband and wife spend in each other's presence that is important; it is the quality of their relationship that is decisive.

14

Quarreling: How to Avoid It

It is difficult for two people, husband and wife, to live in the same house week after week, month after month, and year after year in such close personal relationships with each other without some conflict arising sooner or later. Conflict leads to tensions, and tensions lead to inner smoldering resentment, which can really erupt into open quarreling. When interpersonal conflict results in tensions, the tension *must* be released in order to keep good mental and physical health, or eventually one or both will break under the emotional strain.

Releasing Tensions

To release tensions, conservative Christian thinkers call for opening lines of communication, compromise, and an adjusted toleration—a kind of live-and-help-live policy. Some rather radical thinkers call for a "free expression of feelings" (meaning arguing, quarreling, hostility, and finally, slugging it out). They argue that quarreling releases the tension and that there is healing value in the process of making up after the quarrel. This latter idea sounds more like the behavior of immature children than two mature adults who regard each other as equals.

Judson and Mary Landis oppose quarreling and call for restraint and self-control.[9] They feel that the only possible benefit of quarreling is that it "releases pent-up emotions" and "brings the differences out into the open." The Landises believe there ought to be more constructive ways to do both.

Quarreling produces more tension than it releases. It
widens the rift between husband and wife. In their anger
during a quarrel, both tend to exaggerate their sides of the
argument. Couples are usually ashamed of what they have
said when the quarrel is over. Most decisions made during
quarreling are very questionable. It is impossible for husband and wife to practice quarreling and keep it from their
children. Quarreling has a permanent, harmful impact on
the children's emotional life. The experience is hard for all
persons concerned to forget. Quarreling between husband
and wife tends to spread. Quarreling begets quarreling. The
more quarrels, the more tension, the more inner resentment, the deeper the emotional scars—and the more affection is dulled and declines. And thus, the vicious cycle rolls
on—often into the divorce court.

Doctor Paul Popenoe says, "There are four times a day at
which quarrels are particularly harmful: (1) Around breakfast time . . . . (2) When the husband comes home at
night . . . . (3) After the couple go to bed at night . . . and
(4) any other time." [10]

One couple had a hard-and-fast rule that they would
never quarrel in front of the children. Most of the time they
discovered that when they finally were alone, they couldn't
remember what they wanted to quarrel about! In conversation, neither husband nor wife should make any derogatory
reference to one another's height, size, shape, place of ori-
gin, past mistakes, weaknesses, or relatives.

The Key to Avoiding Quarrels

Assuming husband and wife love one another in the true
sense of love—and that they are committed to basic
spiritual, moral, social, and Christian values as marriage
guidelines—the key to avoiding quarrels is a regularly
planned two-way system of communication. To be effective, this calls for the biblical doctrine of equality. This
means that each feels free to express his deepest feelings

instead of burying them to accumulate and finally to erupt into violent emotional conflict at a later time. One couple, when they had been married one week, sat down across the table and had their first family conference. They discussed such questions as, "How are we doing? What have we done this first week that was good that ought to be continued?" and "What have we done that was not so good and should be avoided in our marriage?" They continued these conferences once a week, and at the end of two years of marriage talked in glowing terms of how these conferences had placed their marriage on solid ground.

A busy medical doctor, on his day and night off from office duties, would build a fire in the fireplace, and he and his wife would sit down in front of the fireplace and talk for one or two hours. The period would always end with a devotional including Bible reading and prayer. This was their night to talk, to plan, to keep lines of communication open, and neither would allow other plans to interrupt that conference.

Doctor Paul Popenoe recommends what he calls a "mensiversary." (*Mens* means *month.*) Whereas an anniversary occurs once per year, a mensiversary would be observed monthly. For example, a couple whose marriage was on June 10 would set aside the tenth of each month to go out together—alone—to their favorite eating place. After a quiet meal they would discuss matters that needed to be planned for the next month, including both the good and not so good experiences of the past month, and how to improve their interpersonal relationships.

We fear that couples who are constantly quarreling may be lazy, or self-centered, or insecure, or immature, or have a lack of imaginative creativity and simple communication organization. In short, they are either not Christian or have drifted from their Christian guidelines and are flowing downstream in a corrupt, permissive culture.

15

Do-It-Yourself Marriage Counseling

Ronald and Evelyn Jarvis had been married nine years. They were college graduates and had two fine children. In their marriage they had followed the line of least resistance, until gradually their happiness had declined and their communication was at minus zero. Evelyn called me (Herbert) long distance and inquired if I would try to help them save their marriage. We set a date for the first appointment. Then she told me she had not told Ronald about possible marriage counseling and was not certain how he would respond. The next day she called back and said Ronald would not agree to counseling. He told her there were two things he would never do, go to a psychiatrist or to a marriage counselor. He said he thought they ought to be able to work out their problems by themselves. Then she asked if there was such a thing as "do-it-yourself" marriage counseling and, if so, could I make some suggestions as to how to go about it.

Let us digress to say that it is foolish for any person to whimsically resolve never to go to see a psychiatrist or marriage counselor. This is about like saying, "I will never go to see a doctor or a dentist." To be sure, there are some incompetent psychiatrists and marriage counselors. There are some inferior doctors and dentists. We cannot reject all of a profession because there are a few weak individuals in it. Although psychiatry and marriage counseling are newer professions than medicine and dentistry, they have been tested and accepted by most of society as necessary for the well-being of husbands and wives, the family, and society. They are here to stay. When we have a sick body or a sick tooth, it is wise to go to a doctor or dentist. When we have a sick mind or a sick marriage, it is wise to go to a competent and responsible psychiatrist, psychologist, or marriage counselor.

First Steps in Self-Counseling

It is possible for a husband and wife, whose marriage is in deep trouble, to improve their relationship and save the marriage, if they are willing to put out the effort necessary. "Do-it-yourself marriage counseling" must involve a healthy two-way communication between husband and wife. They must talk things out in organized, planned conferences. These conferences must be calm, serene, and peaceful. There must be no flights of temper or shouting at each other. Both sides must be stated and understood by each spouse.

One way for couples who are not experienced counselors to bring their problems out in the open is to read together a good book that discusses husband-wife relationships. A visit to a Christian bookstore would help a couple locate some good books. Fortunately, there are dozens of them in print. A pastor would gladly suggest some good books (or consult our reading list in the back of this book). These books discuss the main problems that cause conflicts between husbands and wives, including such subjects as money, in-laws, religion, sex, child care, social problems, insecurity, and immaturity. The purpose of reading these books is to promote communication and wise reasoning about oneself and each other.

Once a book is secured there should be a planned time each day, if possible, when one reads and the other listens. The couple should feel free to comment on what the book says, as it relates to their experiences. During these sessions couples should avoid trying to locate the blame for their problems. This would only encourage further conflict. Rather, they should try to understand one another's feelings and attitudes and carefully examine their own feelings and attitudes. Usually in husband-wife conflict the responsibility is about fifty-fifty, or it may be forty-sixty, or sixty-forty. During the sessions of reading and discussing the book, the couple could set up a few general ground rules—agreeable to both—about their future relationships. Couples do not have to agree on everything to have happiness in marriage. In Christian love, it is possible to disagree without being disagreeable. Yet the more things they can agree on, the better.

If the Conferences Don't Work . . .

If these conferences do not work, and conflict is getting more extreme and tense, a couple would do well to get into their automobile and ride awhile in order to get away from the situation that creates quarreling. It would be even better to hire a responsible baby-sitter, and go to the mountains or seashore, where they can be alone and free from home responsibilities for a couple of days. When they sit down across from each other at a candlelit table in a quiet restaurant, they will realize that there is nothing worth the struggle they are going through. Both should be willing to renew their love and their marriage vows. We recommend such a trip at least twice a year for all married couples. It would tend to promote understanding, happiness, and appreciation for each other.

Put It on Paper

If such a trip does not improve a marriage, and a couple still cannot communicate without shouting at each other in ugly emotional scenes, then we recommend that a couple agree to write out on paper their attitudes and feelings about each other and their marriage. Each would compliment the other by listing every admirable quality they can think of.

There are always many good things that can be said. After the compliments, each one should list (in dignified language) problems and complaints. Take enough time to write the papers in a humble manner designed to promote understanding, goodwill, and reconciliation. At an agreed time the couple would sit down and calmly read each paper. They could flip a coin to decide who reads first. Assuming the wife reads first, her husband would listen and not interrupt the reading. Then the husband would read his paper and his wife would listen and not interrupt.

Final Steps

Then we suggest that they repeat the reading to be sure that they each understand the problems they must face. Next, we recommend that the couple put the two papers together, strike a match and burn them to ashes. At this point, we recommend that the couple separate for a couple of hours. Maybe the husband could go get a haircut, visit with friends, or just take a long walk. During the separation both should concentrate on his or her own weaknesses. Then when back together again *neither husband nor wife should ever bring up or try to refute the negative criticism,* but each should try to correct those attitudes and patterns of behavior that have been bugging the other. By following the above procedure, the couple can each bring their grievances out in the open without an emotional scene. This procedure can work, if both parties want to save their marriage.

Seeing a Marriage Counselor

If this do-it-yourself marriage counseling does not work—and if nothing works—and the worst comes to the worst, we recommend that before going to a lawyer and the divorce court, the couple should agree to go to a responsible Christian marriage counselor. Their own pastor (or a local pastor) may be able to help them. Yet in some cases, it may be better for a pastor *not* to become involved in the ugly details of the problems of his members. In other cases, it may be wise for the pastor to be their marriage counselor. If the pastor feels it's unwise, then certainly he will assist the couple in locating the proper counselor.

If the couple prefers not to involve their pastor in their problems at all, we suggest they write to the following address and ask the organization to recommend a marriage counselor in their area:

> American Association of Marriage
> and Family Counselors
> 225 Yale Avenue
> Claremont, California   91711

If by chance, the American Association of Marriage and Family Counselors cannot help the couple find someone near them, the local family social service agency in larger cities usually has a qualified marriage counselor on the staff. If there is no social service agency in the area, the local county or city Social Welfare office or mental health clinic can usually help.

A couple must have confidence in the marriage counselor selected. They should not put too much importance on prestigious graduate degrees or memberships in professional organizations in selecting a counselor. Some counselors may be trained in psychiatry, psychology, sociology, social work, medicine, or law, but have little to offer a couple in solving their problems and saving their marriage. Sometimes educated people have negative ideas about people and life, and can be indifferent toward strengthening a client's marriage and family life. To be sure, good education and training are valuable, but a marriage counselor should be happily married, a person with unimpeachable Christian character and personality, a person who has a warm, understanding attitude toward a couple and their problems, a person who loves people and enjoys helping them.

Worth the Time and Expense

An out-of-town counselor would involve a call for an appointment, and motel expenses, but the counselor's fee, which could be higher when he has a counseling session with one or both every day, would still be less than the cost of a divorce. The trip out of town together for a week or ten days could be a major factor in saving the marriage. Even if the counseling trip did cost more than a divorce, it is the finest bargain a couple will ever find. Saving a marriage can mean more in noneconomic values than can ever be adequately measured. Breaking a marriage is hard on a couple's self-esteem. It is failing at one of life's major endeavors. No one wants to be a failure. A couple should leave no stone unturned in an effort to save their marriage.

PART III
SEXUAL EQUALITY

16

A Christian Theology of Sex

Many practicing Christians are somewhat familiar with Christian theology on such subjects as God, man, sin, repentance, faith, the Virgin Birth, the Crucifixion, the Resurrection, the Second Coming, stewardship, missions, prayer, et cetera. This is good. The Bible gives details on all these subjects. But the Bible also has much to say about sex. It will probably come as a shock to many people to discover how frequently and frankly the Bible speaks about sex.

Sex is a strong drive in both men and women. We need to admit this to ourselves and make an intelligent effort to understand ourselves and others in light of the true nature and purpose of sex. In the past, many Christian leaders have been largely negative on the subject. We all need to develop a positive Christian theology of sex.

What Does the Bible Have to Say About Sex?

1. *Sex is God's idea.* In Genesis 1:27, we are told that "God created man [mankind] in his own image, in the image of God he created him [mankind]; *male and female he created them*" (*italics ours*). This is the first mention of sex in the Scriptures. Sex was God's idea. In

His infinite wisdom He thought about it. He planned
it. He designed its intricate, orderly system as we
know it. Then He created it. He brought it into active
reality. All of our ideas about sex should rest upon the
fact that sex is *God's idea*.

2. *Sex is to be practiced within marriage.* It was so from
the beginning. "Then Adam had sexual intercourse
with *his wife,* and she conceived and gave birth to a
son . . ." (Genesis 4:1 LB, *italics added*). When
stated positively, the Seventh Commandment, "You
shall not commit adultery" (Exodus 20:14), is simply
saying that sexual intercourse belongs to married persons. Although the early Hebrews practiced some
polygamy, it was not and has never been God's plan.
Monogamy as God's ideal is reflected and defended in
the writings of the wisdom literature (Psalms, Proverbs,
Song of Solomon), in the Old Testament prophets, and
throughout the New Testament.

3. *Sex in marriage is a unitive experience.* "Therefore a
man leaves his father and his mother and cleaves to his
wife, and they become one flesh" (Genesis 2:24). The
husband-wife unity expressed in this passage is repeated and emphasized by both Jesus (Matthew 19:5,
Mark 10:7) and the apostle Paul (1 Corinthians 6:16;
Ephesians 5:31). In sexual intercourse husband and
wife become a unit. They complement and supplement
each other. They fulfill each other. They are a unit in
the sense that a lock and a key are a working unit. A
lock without a key is almost useless. A key without a
lock is equally useless. But a lock and a key together
constitute a valuable working unit. Biblically speaking,
a man without a wife is incomplete; a woman without a
husband is incomplete. Together a man and woman in
marriage make both complete persons into an active
working unit.

Longfellow in *Hiawatha* used the illustration of a

bow and cord. A bow without a cord would be useless. A cord without a bow would be useless. But a bow and a cord together constitutes a working unit that will sling the arrow toward its goal. Thus in describing the husband-wife unity Hiawatha said:

"As unto the bow the cord is,
So unto the man is woman,
Though she bends him, she obeys him,
Though she draws him, yet she follows,
Useless each without the other!"

4. *Sex in marriage is primarily an experience of giving.* "The husband should *give* to his wife her conjugal rights and likewise the wife to her husband" (1 Corinthians 7:3, *italics added*). The word *give* means "to give up to," "to give over to." He gives himself to her. She gives herself to him. In complete abandonment, each surrenders to the other. One flesh is accomplished. Thus in Christian marriage, in the privacy of the bedroom, with doors locked, modesty yields and surrenders to complete self-giving and the joy of possessing each other is realized. Sex in marriage is an experience of giving.

5. *Sex was planned by the Creator as a personal pleasure for marriage.* Christianity has shied away from the Bible concept of personal sexual pleasure in marriage. This has been unfortunate. In Proverbs (5:18, 19) a young man is advised to ". . . rejoice in the wife of your youth. Let her charms and tender embrace satisfy you. Let her love fill you with delight" (LB). The sheer delight of sexual ecstasy and happiness in marriage is the central theme of the Song of Solomon. The language of the Bible concerning sex is dignified and impersonal, but it does not hesitate to spell out in beautiful poetic language the personal pleasure God planned for husband and wife in marriage. Why should Chris-

tians be surprised that our infinite loving God should endow us with the potential for personal sexual pleasure? Let us imagine for a moment that God has created man and woman just as they are, but without their sexual nature. Had he done so, then husband and wife could never completely express their love for each other. God created sex as a physical act of pleasure with spiritual and emotional overtones. Larry Christenson is right when he argues that it is easy to over-spiritualize sex in beautiful philosophical language and ignore the physical pleasure involved. He insists that we ought to refer to sex in marriage as fun.[11]

6. *Sex was planned by the Creator for the purpose of procreation.* After God created man and woman, we read, "And God blessed them, and God said to them, 'Be fruitful and multiply, and fill the earth and subdue it . . .' " (Genesis 1:28). Procreation means creation for and on behalf of another. In their sex life, husband and wife function as God's agents continuing His creative work. They are partners with God in creation. T. B. Maston points out that married couples "who can and should have children and who deliberately and permanently thwart this basic purpose of marriage are violating a fundamental law of marriage." [12] (Of course, this does not refer to couples who cannot have children because of circumstances beyond their control.)

7. *Sex for pleasure and sex for reproduction are two separate systems with two separate functions in the plan of Creation.* The two systems are related to each other, yet they have two separate functions—pleasure and reproduction. We should note that when the Bible talks about sex for pleasure, it does not demand reproduction as a result of the one-flesh union. This is true in the Book of Genesis, in the teachings of Jesus, and the writings of the apostle Paul. The Bible does not say that

sex is for reproduction only. (Detailed evidence concerning sex for pleasure and sex for reproduction as two separate systems and two separate functions is given in *Sexual Understanding Before Marriage*.[13])

8. *Sex in Christian marriage glorifies God.* In 1 Corinthians 6:9–20, Paul is advocating sexual morality and rejecting sexual immorality. He says, ". . . The body is not meant for immorality, but for the Lord . . . . Do you not know that your bodies are members of Christ? Shall I therefore take the members of Christ and make them members of a prostitute? Never! . . . Shun immorality. Every other sin a man commits is outside the body; but the immoral man sins against his own body. Do you not know that your body is a temple of the Holy Spirit within you, which you have from God? You are not your own; you were bought with a price. So glorify God in your body" (1 Corinthians 6:13, 15, 18–20). In this passage Paul strikes a body blow at the immorality of the pagan world in Corinth. But he is careful to point out that sexual intercourse in marriage does not defile our bodies. Rather, it is sacred. It is good. It is a part of the will of God for husband and wife. God dwells in our bodies in the person of the Holy Spirit. Therefore, when husband and wife experience sexual intercourse, God is watching and God is approving (Proverbs 5) through the Holy Spirit. God not only watches and approves, but the experience glorifies God; that is, it achieves, it consummates the one-flesh relationship in accord with His creative purpose.

9. *The misuse and abuse of sex is evil.* There are many biblical terms to indicate the misuse and abuse of sex. The two major terms are *fornication* (premarital sex) and *adultery* (extramarital sex). Some form of Greek *porneia,* translated *fornication* or *fornicator* in the King James Version, occurs thirty-nine times in the New Testament.

Out of seven lists of sins in the writings of Paul, the word *fornication* or *fornicator* is included in five of them (1 Corinthians 5:11, 6:9; Galatians 5:19; Ephesians 5:3; Colossians 3:5) and is first on the list each time. The Seventh Commandment is "Thou shalt not commit adultery" (Exodus 20:14). Jesus put fornication and adultery in the same class when He said, ". . . everyone who looks at a woman lustfully [with the thought of sexual intercourse with her] has already committed adultery with her in his heart" (Matthew 5:28). The "everyone" includes both men and women, both married and unmarried. Thus Jesus is saying that sexual intercourse of unmarried people (fornication) is as evil as extramarital sexual intercourse (adultery). Note that sexual sins consist of both an inward condition of the heart and/or the outward act. Paul associates fornication and adultery with such other sins as hate, drunkenness, murder, et cetera, and says, "I warn you . . . that those who do such things shall not inherit the kingdom of God" (Galatians 5:21). Paul teaches that our bodies participate in our spiritual union with Christ (this is why we refer to sex as being sacred) and that sexual promiscuity (fornication and adultery) violates that spiritual union.

10. *All sexual sins may be forgiven.* The idea that there are different levels of sins such as small, medium, and great may be a part-truth in the sight of God. Certainly social law makes such distinctions. But all sin is sin in the sense that it is wrong. It is against God, His laws, His will, His person. There is only one way to get rid of sin—repentance, confession, and petition to God for forgiveness. Cheating on an examination as well as premarital and extra-marital sex are forgiven through the same simple procedure. Some people have the idea that sexual sins are more evil than other sins and thus it is more difficult to receive forgiveness for them. There

is no Scripture to justify this idea. The Scriptures teach, ". . . though your sins are like scarlet [fornication, adultery, and other sexual sins] they shall be as white as snow" (Isaiah 1:18).

Needed: A Total Christian Theology of Sex

These ten doctrinal statements are only some of the total biblical doctrines related to sex. Yes, it will perhaps come as a shock to many people to discover how frequently and how frankly the Bible discusses sex. Evangelical Christianity needs to stress a total "Christian theology of sex" as related to family life in a balanced emphasis with the other Christian doctrines, such as the nature of God, man, the Bible, sin, salvation, and eternal life.

The American family is now experiencing a major sexual crisis. This crisis has not originated within the family circle. It is largely the result of external ideas and forces originating from our drifting, decaying, sensual culture. A sexual revolution is here! It is real! It is social and moral anarchy! It could annihilate our civilized family and community organization. Never does mankind dig its own grave so deep as when he worships sex as a god and ignores the total rights and needs of persons and the plan of the Creator for their lives. A wise emphasis on the Christian theology of sex is necessary to strengthen family life, so that society can resist the immoral forces that seem determined to misuse and abuse one of God's greatest blessings—human sexuality.

17

Paul's Description of Sexual Equality: 1 Corinthians 7:1–5

Paul's description of husband-wife sexual equality in 1 Corinthians 7:1–6 is best understood in light of his reasoning in chapters 5 and 6, where he insists that the pagan sexual immorality of Corinth was incompatible with and contrary to Christian living. In Paul's list of sins he names the sexual sins of Corinth including adultery, fornication, and homosexuality (*see* 5:11). Before they became Christians, many, if not all, of the Corinthian church members had been guilty of these sensual sins. But they are now Christians. They have been "washed," "sanctified," and "justified" in the name of Jesus Christ. Therefore, Paul calls for personal, sexual purity in their lives. He tells them that they are to use their bodies to serve God, admonishes them that sexual perversion defiles their bodies, which belong to Christ, and teaches them that they must glorify God with their bodies (1 Corinthians 6:13–20).

Paul's Positive Discussion

Following this negative discussion in which Paul condemns sexual promiscuity, and in response to the letter he had received from the Corinthian church, he launched into a *positive* discussion in chapter 7 of how Christian husbands and wives should use their sexual nature. After he briefly states that it is good for a man "not to touch" a woman (verse 1), that is, remain single and abstain from sexual intercourse, he shifts to the positive approach and comes to grips with the reality of the sexual nature of men and women. But because of the temptation to immorality (premarital sexual relations), he recommended marriage.

All of Christendom needs to come face to face with Paul's statement, "But because of the temptation to sexual intercourse before marriage . . ." (*see* verse 2). Why don't we all frankly admit that sex is strong and central in all of our lives—both male and female, Christian and non-Christian, learned and simple, rich and poor, upper class and lower class? The Creator created us thus. Each person should admit this to himself or herself. There is no reason why we should be ashamed of our strong, turbulent sex drive! Instead we should be thankful to God for it. The Christian community has avoided far too long an open confrontation with the problem of how to control and direct this divinely created sex drive. Our silence has been unchristian, cowardly, and sometimes deadly. We have abandoned many fine men and women to the mercy of their own lusts, anxieties, and guilt feelings.

Sexual Equality

The apostle Paul did not hesitate to face the reality of human sexuality. In verses 3, 4, and 5, he gives explicit details. The biblical concept of husband-wife equality is here applied to the husband's and wife's sexual nature. These verses are literally saturated with the concept of equality. Because of the temptation to premarital sex, Paul says, ". . . *each* man should have *his own* wife and *each* woman should have *her own* husband" (*italics ours*). This is monogamy. All other man-instituted forms of marriage, such as polygamy, polyandry, concubinage, and group marriage are rejected. This is in accord with the original plan of God who said, "It is not good that the man should be alone . . ." (Genesis 2:18).

In verse 3 Paul elaborates on the sexual equality of

monogamy. "The husband should give to his wife her conjugal rights, and likewise the wife to her husband." This could be translated literally, "The husband should meet his wife's sexual needs and the wife should meet her husband's sexual needs." Note the husband's responsibility to his wife is stated first. This (verse 3) assumes sexual intercourse and orgasm. It is not the responsibility of the wife to meet her own sexual needs. It is not the responsibility of the husband to meet his own sexual needs. Rather it is the husband's responsibility to meet his wife's sexual needs, and it is the responsibility of the wife to meet her husband's sexual needs. In this manner the total needs of both are met, and one flesh is realized. Every succeeding act of intercourse continues, sustains, and renews this one-flesh unity.

In verse 4 Paul continues, "For the wife does not rule over her own body but the husband does . . . ." Thus a wife's body does not belong to her. It belongs to her husband and he *rules over it*. But ladies, wait! Do not be alarmed! We are in the middle of Paul's sentence. He continues, ". . . *likewise* the husband does not rule over his own body, but the wife does" (*italics added*). Thus a husband's body does not belong to him. It belongs to his wife and *she rules over it*. Paul repeated these details, like a carpenter clinching the nail on the other side, in order to emphasize the sexual equality of husbands and wives. This is in line with the Creator's plan for husband and wife to become "one flesh." Sexual responsibilities of both husband and wife are parallel, reciprocal, and equal. How strange that we have never heard a sermon or read a book that calls attention to the fact that *wives rule over their husbands' bodies!*

In this interpersonal sexual equality between husband and wife, both have sexual needs and desires. Each depends upon the other to fulfill his or her needs. Neither can be passive, both must be active. He gives himself to her.

She gives herself to him. He becomes aware of his total nature and his wife's total nature. She becomes aware of her total nature and her husband's total nature. This knowledge is at the highest, deepest, and broadest possible level of awareness. This one flesh is a total relationship of the whole person of the husband to the whole person of his wife. It is a total relationship of the whole person of the wife to the whole person of her husband.

The Urgent Nature of Sexuality

In verse 5 Paul further emphasizes his concept of sexual equality and the urgent nature of human sexuality. He says, "Do not refuse *one another* [italics ours] except by agreement for a season, that you may devote yourselves to prayer: but then come together again [in sexual intercourse] lest Satan tempt you through lack of self-control." Here Paul states negatively what he had said positively in verse 3. He is saying that it is normal for husband and wife to continue to meet each other's sexual needs. They are not to refuse one another except by agreement "for a season," that they may devote themselves to prayer.

In light of the context (1) the urgency of the sex drive and (2) the avoidance of fornication, this has to be understood to be for a short season. At the end of the short season they are to "come together again": that is, they are to resume sexual intercourse, meeting each other's sexual needs. Verse 5 is completed with a repetition of verse 2, "lest Satan tempt you through lack of self-control." To those who imply that Paul had a very low and weak concept of human nature, because it is difficult to control one's sexual nature, we would reply, "Don't look now, but your assumption that sex is evil, which you have been trying to hide, is showing." Paul was simply and honestly facing up to the nature of human sexuality as it was divinely created and outlining methods to utilize it to the glory of God.

Overwhelming Proof of Sexual Equality

The language in those four verses describing husband-wife sexual equality is overwhelming. *"Each"* should have his or her *"own"* spouse. *Each* should meet the *other's* sexual needs. *Each* rules over the body and the sexuality of the *other*. The couple is not to *"refuse one another."* The only exception Paul sees is an agreed abstinence for prayer. After the short period of prayer is passed, they are to *"come together"* again. This passage confirms that (1) husbands and wives are sexual equals in the plan of the Creator; (2) sex, as such, is good and not evil; and, (3) that, in marriage, deep spirituality and a good sex life belong together.

18

The Christian View of Masculinity

The traditional concept of masculinity has called for the male to be self-confident, aggressive, bold, daring, fearless, tough, rugged, venturesome, and often hostile and reckless—a sort of community John Wayne! He was to drink alcoholic beverages, use drugs, use profane language, and fight at the drop of a hat. He was to have no sympathy, empathy, compassion, or tenderness. He was not to be bashful or modest. Sex was his prerogative, and he was to use women freely as objects to satisfy his drives. A continuous, exploitative, playboy sex life was necessary to support his ever-sagging ego. In the family, he was to be the breadwinner, handle all financial matters, and be absolute authority over his family. It was not his responsibility to care for the children in the home, and under no circumstances was he to stoop so low as to do housework.

Cause and Effect of Such Gobbledygook

This image is composed of pure gobbledygook. It is a world of futile, fleeting fantasy—unrelated to the world of human reality. Those who imitate the traditional masculine image are mentally and emotionally sick, grasping at straws, trying to protect their immature and insecure egos.

This masculine image grew out of our cultural background, including the abnormal conditions of the western frontier, and the keeping of the western-frontier image alive through western movies and western stories in pulp magazines, our cultural patriarchal philosophy, and the self-centered nature of sinful, frail human beings.

The traditional role of male masculinity is loaded with serious and major human problems. Gary Collins points out that most men do not really fit into this image, simply because their real, human needs are not met by the behavior patterns of the image. He says:

> Deep inside men know that they often are sensitive, passive, gentle, insecure, and needing to depend on others—the very antithesis of the popular definition of masculinity. Some males simply do not have athletic abilities or bulging muscles (except around the stomach). They want the freedom to express love openly and even to cry (as Jesus did).[14]

Many of those who are determined to follow the traditional image soon fall by the wayside in a sad and early disillusionment. Those who manage to survive find to their sorrow, that with the passing of years, the need for this egotistical behavior of men in their twenties fades, crumbles, and disintegrates. They are often left lonely, unhappy, and on the mercy of society.

The True Christian Concept

What is the Christian concept of male masculinity? A man following the Christian masculine image recognizes that he is a person created in the image of God with physical, emotional, and spiritual needs. He understands that these needs can be met only in Jesus Christ. He recognizes he has certain abilities, talents, and skills and lacks certain abilities, talents, and skills. He recognizes that other men and women have his same needs and skills. Since all people are created after the same pattern (the image of God), he recognizes that they are his equals in the plan of Creation. He recognizes his own strong sexuality, and directs it into moral channels which respect the sexuality of all other persons. He puts meeting the sexual rights and needs of his wife before his own. He is concerned about his wife's development as a total person. He is anxious to help his wife reach her life goals along with his efforts to reach his life goals. He is more interested in his duties and responsibilities to his wife and his family than he is in his personal rights and authority. He must realize that husbands and wives must operate on the level of equals and partners in the channels of God's grace. He is humble, thoughtful, and compassionate.

He is *not* a spineless weakling, but a strong, bold, decisive, honest leader who is tender, gentle, and kind in human relationships. He presents aggressive and efficient family and community leadership. His relationship with his children reflects a thoughtful, moral example, relaxed play, empathetic understanding, and genuine love. He openly resists evil and is concerned about his own spiritual growth. He uses as his life guidelines the Ten Commandments, the Sermon on the Mount, and the simple teachings of the Man of Galilee.

> His life is long and happy because he does not hang around with evil men nor scoff at the plans of God. He delights in doing the things God wants him to do. Day and night he meditates on God's law. He is like a tree planted by the river bank that bears abundant fruit every season.
>
> Psalms 1:1–3 (a paraphrase of LB)

Guidelines for Christian Masculinity

Gary Collins outlines the following series of stable guidelines that sum up the nature of Christian masculinity, that can help the male who would be truly masculine and that leaves room for individual differences and cultural changes:

First, to be truly masculine is to be a follower and imitator of Jesus Christ.

Second, true masculinity consists of overtly resisting the devil and growing as a man of God.

Third, the truly masculine male recognizes and accepts his unique abilities and weaknesses.

Fourth, true masculinity involves the freedom to acknowledge one's sexuality.

Fifth, the truly masculine male is sensitive to the needs of women and alert to his responsibilities as husband and father.[15]

Any man anywhere can fit into this image. He will find that it meets his total needs. This image is not a thin spiderweb of passing fantasy, but a network of values—strong as steel cords—that grows increasingly stronger with the passing of the years.

19

The Christian View of Femininity

One hundred years ago the concept of femininity in our society emphasized woman as the wife and mother. She was to care for the children, do all of the household tasks, make clothes for the family, repair torn and worn-out clothes, prepare all meals, and help grow the food. She was to be modest and shy, and sympathetic to her children and husband. (Good, so far.) But she did not need an education. She was to keep out of politics. She was not allowed to vote. She had little or nothing to say about the financial side of the home. She was supposed to submit to all of her husband's sexual advances, but she was not supposed to enjoy sex. (To do so would have been unladylike.) She was not supposed to make decisions except minor ones involving her limited family role. Her husband was the head of the house and the final authority. Her social life was almost nonexistent.

Source of Traditional View

Some of this traditional cultural image of women is composed of mere gobbledygook. Historically, it grew out of the patriarchal ideas of ancient civilizations (Jews, Greeks, Romans, Chinese, Arabs, and so forth). The self-centered ego, the robust physical strength and sex drive, and the frail, sinful nature of human beings gradually caused men to exalt themselves and push women into an inferior status, devoid of freedom, and into a life of subjection to men and society. In the past, in many ways it resembles servitude and slavery. Some form of it still exists in many nations yet, today. Unfortunately some remnants of it remain active in our society.

This traditional role of the female is loaded with serious human problems. Women simply do not fit into the limitations of this restricted human cage, because women's real human needs are not met by the behavioral patterns of the image. The image puts women in a limited world of confinement and captivity, with little freedom of self-expression, self-development and self-fulfillment as a person created in the image of God. It leaves women lonely, unhappy and often at the mercy of little tyrants who parade as their husbands. This image is strictly cultural. It is largely unchristian and unscientific.

The True Christian Concept

Now, what *is* the Christian concept of femininity? At this point it is necessary to distinguish between the patriarchal nature of the early Hebrew culture in the Old Testament and the teachings of Jesus. Jesus' teachings, His attitudes, and His behavior toward women dealt a body blow to this primitive patriarchalism. (*See* Appendix). The early church fathers likewise distorted the teachings of Jesus, as Gladys Hunt says:

> . . . Tertullian spoke of women as "the mother of all ills." Chrysostom wrote of women as "a natural temptation and desirable calamity, a deadly fascination," almost as if woman were designed by Satan instead of created in the image of God. Thomas Aquinas betrayed his prejudice by agreeing with Aristotle that "woman is a misbegotten male," a statement that hardly honors God's creation. St. (sic) Augustine agreed with the Greco-Roman tradition that a woman's sole function was procreation. In fact, I find the writings of the early church fathers on this

subject appalling! And we are still saddled today with remnants of this male interpretation of theology.[16]

A woman needs personal fulfillment. As Beardsley and Spry say, "Fulfillment does not come from pleasing our husbands . . . from having the best behaved kids on the block . . . from keeping an immaculate house, being a gourmet cook, or the best-dressed or the most well-read woman." [17] Today the Christian concept of femininity and fulfillment still emphasizes woman as wife and mother (marriage and mother are not dirty words), but rejects the cultural limitations and restrictions of the patriarchal teachings. Husband and wife must regard each other as equals and treat each other with mutual esteem.

A wife is to be treated as an individual—a person—created in the image of God with many creative potentialities. She needs to be right with God, through repentance from sin and receiving Christ as her personal Savior. She needs social acceptance and self-expression. She needs to love her husband and be loved by him. She should be concerned about meeting the needs and rights of her husband first, her children second, her parents third, but she should also be concerned about herself—her spiritual and mental growth, personality development, and social responsibilities. By systematic organization, ingenuity, and old-fashioned happy work, she can meet her family and community responsibilities and, at the same time, can fully develop her mind, personality, and spiritual potential. Thousands of women have done so.

The Essence of Femininity

In the final analysis, however, the essence of femininity is that mysterious aura about a woman that distinguishes her from a man. To be equal does not mean that male and female are to be alike. It is our opinion that the present vogue of the unisex look in clothing is only a passing fad, because it violates the nature of mankind as God created us. It's the subtle differences that make a woman attractive to a man—the soft, round contour of her body, the "skin you love to touch," the gentle voice, the graceful movements. The Creator made her thus, and wise is the woman who dresses to accentuate, not eliminate, these natural endowments of God.

The effort to make oneself attractive to the opposite sex will be tempered by modesty in a Christian woman. Modesty is a virtue that should characterize both sexes, but it is especially important for a woman to realize that since a man is sexually aroused by visual stimuli, she must be careful in her dress (or lack of it), physical movements, and so forth, not to do anything that would appear to be an open invitation to sexual advances.

True femininity or female beauty is an outward manifestation of an inner beauty that develops when a woman is at peace with God and herself, who has found complete fulfillment as a person, spiritually, mentally, and socially.

20

Cultural Sexual Myths Vs. Christian and Scientific Facts

God created man and woman in His own image and instructed the man to leave his parents and cleave to his wife and to become one flesh. Thus God created marriage as a permanent social institution. Jesus, in His teachings, reemphasized the Genesis account of the one man-one woman, husband-wife relationship. The apostle Paul not only emphasized the one-flesh relationship, but spelled out considerable details in 1 Corinthians, chapter 7. The Book of Proverbs (chapter 5) and the Song of Solomon further spelled out, in beautiful language, the husband-wife relationship.

It is our purpose now to spell out in further detail the husband-wife one-flesh relationship in simple, modern language using dignified, scientific, and biblical terms. We want to help husbands and wives in their own interpersonal relationships. Also we want to help husbands and wives to move in the direction of being counselors to other married people who need help. We want to break down inhibitions that are not scientific or Christian, and set forth concepts that are both scientific *and* Christian. We want to separate fact from fiction. We propose to do this by comparing past and present cultural sexual myths with Christian and scientific sexual facts.

The Double-*B* Books

We will be using information from what we call "the double-*B* books, that is, the *Bible* and *biology* (physiology) books. God used men to write the Bible, but He was the ultimate author through the process of inspiration. Men write biology books. How do they do it? They simply observe the intricate details of how God created man and woman in His image, and then write down these findings in biology books. Therefore God is the ultimate Author of both the Bible and biology books. Hence, when we rest our thinking about human sexuality on the double-*B* books, we get a comfortable feeling of maximum authority.

Definition of a Myth

A myth is a traditional story or idea that has grown up in a culture about a world view or about human life and behavior that is false, yet is believed and practiced as if it were truth. Many myths have grown up around sexual behavior in our culture. They are difficult to dislodge, in order that truth may prevail. This is especially true among false religions that have a habit of connecting sexual practices with religious rituals or rejecting sexuality as being antireligious. Myths often pack much political, social, and religious muscle. It is very difficult to uproot and defeat them.

Let us now examine fifteen cultural myths about sex life in marriage and expose their false and deceptive teachings.

Myth 1

Sex is man's prerogative. Woman should remain passive. The primitive idea that wives should be passive in married sexual life is in complete violation of the clear teachings in 1 Corinthians 7:3. The passage is saying that women have a definite need for regular sexual experience in marriage, and it seems to assume that regular sexual orgasms in a sexual experience with her husband are due her, and are necessary to complete the unitive nature of her marriage.

Biological and sociological research verifies the sexual needs of women. Most authorities suggest that wives need a sexual release on the average of twice per week. My (Herbert) own research of 151 couples indicates that the wives want to have regular sexual experiences with their husbands on an average of once every 3.2 days. Sixty-one percent of the wives wanted a sexual experience as often or more often than did their husbands. Thus the traditional concept that married women are not really interested in sex life and should remain passive is not in accord with biblical *or* scientific reality.

Myth 2

Man is more sexual than woman. It is in order to ask what is meant by the word *more.* If by *more* sexual we are referring to a man's sexual timing from the time sexual stimulation begins until he experiences a sexual orgasm, then we might say that man is more sexual than woman. Most young men can be stimulated to orgasm very quickly, some within one minute or less. On the other hand, woman's timing from beginning stimulation to orgasm may be as long as ten or fifteen minutes, or longer. Of course, on some occasions, it may be as little as five minutes or less.

But can we rightly say that man is more sexual because of his quick timing? Other factors are involved that should be considered. For example, many women, as they mature in married life can learn to experience "multiple orgasms," that is, in one period of fifteen or twenty minutes they may experience two, three, four, or more orgasms. This is normal for some women in marriage. When a man experiences one orgasm, some time must pass—several hours or even longer—before he is ready for another. Therefore if we are considering multiple orgasms, we would have to say that woman is more sexual than man. Also, after husband and wife reach age fifty-five or sixty, frequently wives want and need sexual experiences more often than their husbands.

Thus, when all evidence is considered, it is necessary to conclude that neither man nor woman is more sexual than the other. It would be fair to say that the Creator created them as sexual equals. It is true that they respond differently under different circumstances, but this does not make either the husband or the wife superior or inferior sexually.

Myth 3

Many women are frigid and cannot respond sexually. It is a fact that approximately 10 percent of wives do not respond sexually, but 90 percent do, in varying degrees. But is it accurate to say that the 10 percent are frigid and that they cannot respond sexually? No! Some of the 10 percent of women who do not respond have been taught that sex is evil, and they believe it. Of course with these mental and emotional attitudes, a woman would not respond sexually. Other women who marry when they are very young are simply uneducated concerning sexual attitudes and techniques in marriage. They do not know the nature of their own sexual need or how to meet it. Neither do their young husbands. Therefore, under these circumstances, these women do not respond sexually. In both cases, it is wrong to say that the women are frigid, meaning that it is impossible for them to respond sexually. The reason they do not respond sexually is that they either think that sex is evil, or they are simply uneducated. When marriage counselors remove these two blocks standing in the way of sexual response, these so-called frigid women learn to respond normally. Hence we can safely say there are no frigid women. (See further discussion of this myth in chapter 22).

Myth 4

Sex is for reproduction only. This myth has a sad and sordid history. Unfortunately, in the past, thousands of otherwise fine people have advocated sex for reproduction only. Our Creator created man and woman so that healthy couples could reproduce approximately every ten or twelve months. At the same time, He created them so that they need a one-flesh sexual experience approximately twice per week. Also there is abundant evidence that the Creator created both man and woman with two separate systems, (1) the reproductive system and (2) the sex-for-pleasure system. Just as He created male and female with a respiratory system and a circulatory system, so He created them with these two separate sexual systems having two separate functions. They are related, yet they are separate.[18]

Myth 5

Husband and wife should not see each other naked. This myth is in direct conflict with the Scripture, "Therefore a man leaves his father and his mother and cleaves to his wife, and they become one flesh. And the man and his wife were both naked, and were not ashamed" (Genesis 2:24, 25). Every marriage counselor is acquainted with cases where husband and wife who have lived together several years, some who have children, and have not seen each other naked. This is often the result of false teaching from parents in childhood. It is obvious that most such marriages are troubled with excess problems and often end in divorce. These couples are in need of help from a competent counselor.

Myth 6

Husband and wife should not touch each other's genital organs. This myth is a carry-over from past ideas that sex is evil except for procreation. The Scriptures in the Song of Solomon directly contradict this myth. The Song of Solomon is composed of beautiful poetry in dignified language describing the sexual pleasures between a young husband and wife. In chapter 2:6 and also 8:3 we have the following sentence: "O that his left hand were under my head, and that his right hand embraced me!" The word *embrace* could easily be translated *fondle* or *stimulate*. If one will visualize the experience and body position of the young husband and wife as it is described in these passages, it is obvious that the young wife, thought to be imprisoned by an Eastern king and refusing to be his wife, is wishing to be with her husband, and longing for him to stimulate her genital organs with his fingers in a mutual love experience.

From the biological point of view, it is an accepted scientific fact that the female clitoris must be stimulated in order for a wife to experience all that God meant for her to experience in the one-flesh relationship. Furthermore, it is positively known that the male penis does not directly touch or stimulate the female clitoris in sexual intercourse. Therefore, the only logical conclusion to be drawn is that the Creator planned the one-flesh relationship to include the touching, fondling, and stimulating of the wife's genitalia. In this process of lovemaking, it is normal to assume that the Creator's plan included lovemaking; it is normal to assume that the Creator's plan also included the wife's touching, fondling, and stimulating her husband's genital organs.

Myth 7

The wife should not tell her husband the type of stimulation that she needs. The wife should not tell him what he is doing wrong. She must not correct him. This myth is a deduction from historical patriarchalism, that is, man is the authority in the family and sex is man's prerogative. Unfortunately, some wives wait ten or twenty years to get up the courage to tell their husbands what they are doing wrong and what she needs. One of the most important ingredients in sexual happiness in marriage that flows from the doctrine of sexual equality is that there must be detailed reciprocal communication between husband and wife during their one-flesh love relationships. (For further discussion on communication, see chapter 12.)

Myth 8

Only young women with 36-24-36 measurements are sexy. The centerfold of *Playboy* magazine displays a nude girl approximately twenty years of age whose measurements are supposed to be 36-24-36. It is assumed that such girls are the most sensual. This is contrary to scientific fact. We used to say that women reach their sexual peak at age twenty-eight or twenty-nine. Now, marriage specialists are saying that women do not actually reach their sexual peak until thirty-five or forty-five. Although the average young woman, under normal circumstances, can have good marriage sexual adjustment at age twenty, she can continue to improve in sexual capacity until age thirty-five to forty-five. Yet from age twenty to age forty-five, women decline in the beauty of their bodies. Hence at age forty-five, although she may not win a *Playboy* beauty contest, the average woman is more efficient sexually than at age twenty. And furthermore, the average married woman, age fifty or sixty, may be more efficient sexually than at age twenty. Efficient sexual adjustment is the result of a spiritual, emotional, and social growth relationship between a husband and wife who love each other in a total commitment. Their age or body measurements have little or nothing to do with it.

Myth 9

There are two kinds of female orgasms: (1) a clitoral orgasm; and, (2) a vaginal orgasm. It is assumed that the clitoral orgasm is shallow and not intense, whereas the vaginal orgasm is assumed to be a deep and intense experience. This concept of two types of orgasms originated largely with Freudian psychoanalysts. During the 1950s and 1960s there was a major debate among marriage specialists concerning the nature of female orgasms. Opponents of Freud insisted there was only one type of female orgasm, and it was a clitoral orgasm. This debate came to a head at The

American Association of Marriage and Family Counselors in Chicago in 1965. The subject of that conference was The Female Orgasm. At that meeting William E. Masters and Virginia Johnson reported publicly on their research and were questioned thoroughly by the members of the conference. Masters took the position that there are no special nerve endings in the vaginal passage other than normal nerve endings found elsewhere inside the body cavity. He stated that the special nerve endings are in the female clitoris, and that the clitoris is the external trigger that sets off female arousal and orgasm. Thus Masters kindly but firmly insisted that there was only one kind of female orgasm—the clitoral orgasm.

This is the position that is accepted today by most scholars. They affirm that the clitoris is the female transmitter and conductor of sexual sensations. It is understood that the intensity of female orgasms may vary from person to person and vary according to circumstances in the same individual. This raised the following question: How do we explain the fact that a few wives can experience orgasms in intercourse without any direct stimulation of the clitoris, since the penis in intercourse does not contact the clitoris directly? The usual reply is that the clitoris is surrounded by and in close proximity to the labia minora (minor lips). During the movement of sexual intercourse the penis moves the labia minora and the labia minora touches and moves the clitoris, which gives sufficient stimulation for the wife to experience orgasm. To this explanation we must add that other factors become a part of the sexual process, such as emotional, psychological, and spiritual love commitment. Yet it needs to be emphasized that there is nothing wrong sexually with wives who cannot experience orgasm without some direct manual stimulation of the clitoris. In fact, the majority of women are in this group.

Myth 10

Husbands and wives must both reach orgasm during sexual intercourse. Helen Caplan, physician and psychiatrist, states that the idea that a woman must have all sexual orgasms in intercourse is a myth. The evidence indicates that a majority of women cannot do so, and unless they have had specific counseling the majority would probably be larger. The details of how to handle this problem are discussed at length in *Sexual Happiness in Marriage,* chapter 5.[19] Christian marriage counselors interpret the biblical term *one flesh* from the physical point of view, not necessarily referring to orgasms by one or both partners. Marriage counselors recommend that couples experiment and try to learn to reach orgasms during intercourse. However, those women who cannot should not feel that they are abnormal or lacking in sexual capacity.

Myth 11

Husband and wife must have orgasms simultaneously in sexual intercourse. Only a small percentage of couples learn to have simultaneous orgasms most of the time. They are usually people who have had good pre-marriage and marriage counseling. Simultaneous orgasms are nearly impossible for most couples. Some couples succeed occasionally by accident. The biological evidence seems to be that the Creator's plan for male and female one-flesh relationships did not include simultaneous orgasms. For example, during the male orgasm in intercourse, he must cease movement. On the other hand, during the female orgasm she must have continued movement and stimulation throughout the orgasm. Modern marriage counselors suggest that it is well for couples to experiment and move in the direction of experiencing simultaneous orgasms for the sake of variety. Details on how to make progress in this direction are given in *Sexual Happiness in Marriage,* chapter 5.[20] However, couples who never succeed in having simultaneous orgasms should not feel that they are sexually deficient in any way.

Myth 12

Husband and wife should never concentrate on themselves during their sexual experiences. It is a fact that while a wife is being aroused by her husband to an orgasm, she needs to concentrate on herself much of the time. This does not mean that she cannot give some attention to her husband. Her concentration on self is not selfishness. This an experienced husband understands. Likewise, there are some husbands who tend to be slow in their sexual arousal to orgasm (especially in life's later years) and need to concentrate on themselves. This does not mean selfishness. It does not violate 1 Corinthians 7:3, 4. Experienced couples understand that self-concentration is necessary on the part of both husband and wife at certain times in the relationship. Thus they lovingly and gladly cooperate with each other.

Myth 13

All masturbation is sinful. Masturbation has traditionally been considered evil under any and all circumstances. Since this is a major problem for many Christians, especially young people, the subject has been hush-hush far too long. It needs to be dealt with openly in line with reality and valid Christian principles. We believe that masturbation, as such, is neither good nor bad. Whether or not it is evil depends upon the motives, the frequency, and possible guilt feelings or other adverse psychological effects.

Because of the bad connotations of the term *masturbation,* we would like to replace it with the term *self-release.* Self-release more accurately defines the practice: the act of using one's own hands and fingers to stimulate one's own genital organs in order to release sexual tension through orgasm.

Let us first consider some facts about self-release:

1. The Bible does not deal with this problem. Genesis 38:8–11 sometimes is quoted as a condemnation of self-release. Actually Onan was not practicing self-release. He had sexual intercourse with Tamar but withdrew before orgasm to avoid making her pregnant. Onan was punished by God because he defied the Hebrew law, which required him to marry his deceased brother's wife to produce offspring for his brother. Likewise, "abusers of themselves with mankind" (1 Corinthians 6:9 KJV) is referring to homosexuality rather than self-release.

2. There is no evidence that occasional self-release is harmful to health. Medical science has dispelled the myth that the practice of self-release will cause sterility, insanity, epilepsy, blindness, or early death. In fact, Butler and Lewis, in discussing the need for self-release to relieve sexual tension when sexual intercourse in marriage is not possible, have said that "total abstinence from sexual activity can be tension-producing, and may result in impotence in men and loss of lubrication as well as vaginal shape in women." [21] This would seem to indicate that the sex organs, like any other part of the body, may slowly lose their ability to perform if not used over a long period of time.

3. Self-release resolves sexual tensions and thus may reduce temptation to fornication or adultery. Certainly we would agree that the practice of self-release on a limited scale as a means of self-control is preferable to promiscuity or marital infidelity.

In *Sexual Understanding Before Marriage* the problem of self-release for single young people is thoroughly discussed.[22] Here we are concerned with the question of whether self-release is ever justified after marriage. Certainly the practice of self-release by one or both partners in preference to sexual intercourse violates the sacred marriage relationship and is therefore evil. If such practice is accompanied by fantasy of sex relations with someone other than one's spouse this is adultery (*see* Matthew 5:28). Even if not accompanied by adulterous fantasy, it is abnormal behavior. Something is seriously wrong when "sheer physical release is selfishly chosen over the personal challenges of lovemaking." [22a]

What if one spouse refuses to have sexual intercourse? Under such circumstances occasional self-release may be necessary to avoid the temptation to infidelity. What if both couples desire sexual intercourse but circumstances make it impossible? When couples cannot have intercourse just before and after childbirth, or during long periods of illness, we recommend interstimulation rather than self-release. The husband and wife stimulate each other to orgasms without sexual intercourse. This can be a pleasurable, shared experience that gives expression to love for each other during the period when they cannot have normal sex relations.

However, when couples have to be away from each other for a long period of time, self-release is a perfectly normal way to meet one another's sexual need. During this experience each would be prayerfully thinking about the other, thanking God for each other, and praying that God will help them remain faithful to each other. Although tension is released, sometimes a deep feeling of loneliness may follow. This letdown feeling should not be interpreted as guilt but rather a realization that self-release is a poor substitute for sexual intercourse which involves much more than release of physical sexual tension.

Myth 14

Sexual oral contact between husband and wife is evil. Since the publication of Herbert's book *Sexual Happiness in Marriage* ten years ago, he has received approximately one hundred letters from all over the United States and some from Canada and Europe, asking questions about sex in marriage. At least one half of those letters were from practicing Christians asking if oral-genital contact in marriage is a violation of Christian teachings. Most all couples who come to his office for marriage counseling ask him about oral sex as related to Christian morals. This is another problem that has been swept under the rug far too long. Truth and reality call for Christians to speak out on this subject.

What is meant by oral sex? Tim and Beverly LaHaye describe it as follows:

> Two words are used to describe oral sex. In *fellatio* the woman receives the male penis into her mouth in order to stimulate the glans penis with her lips and tongue, *cunnilingus* is the act of the male stimulating the woman with his mouth over her vulva area, usually with his tongue on her clitoris. Both forms of oral sex can bring an orgasm if prolonged.[23]

Is oral-genital contact between husband and wife a violation of Christian teachings? The best reply is probably *yes* and *no*. Mrs. Shirley Rice, a marriage counselor on the staff of the Tabernacle Church of Norfolk, Virginia, in discussing technique in husband-wife sex relations, says:

> There is no part of the body which is improper to use—to caress with the lips, the tongue or the hands. Anything is permissible as long as it is not offensive to either party and affords mutual pleasure and satisfaction. Each would certainly refrain from anything that would be offensive to the other, though many inhibitions would be removed with the knowledge that this sort of love-making between man and wife is holy and pleasing to God.[24]

Ed and Gaye Wheat, in discussing the subject, say:

> Oral sex (mouth to genital) is a matter which con-
> cerns only the husband and wife involved. If both of
> you enjoy it and find it pleasant, then it may properly
> fit into your lovemaking practices. If either partner
> has any hesitancy about it, however, it will add little
> to the pleasure of the relationship and should be dis-
> continued.[25]

The LaHayes, in discussing oral sex state that in their
research:

> . . . Of Christian doctors we surveyed, 73 per-
> cent felt it was acceptable for a Christian couple as
> long as both partners enjoyed it; 27 percent did not
> approve of it. To our amazement, 77 percent of the
> ministers felt it was acceptable, and 23 percent did
> not . . . .[26]

In reply to couples who ask in conference or by letter
about the appropriateness of oral sex in Christian marriage,
we usually say that since the Bible is silent on the subject,
we have to be guided by two basic Christian principles: Oral
sex is sinful (1) when one spouse forces it on the other
against his or her will; and (2) when it is substituted regularly for sexual intercourse. On the other hand, oral sex can
be appropriate in Christian marriage when (1) it is occasionally used for variety in short periods during the love play
arousal experience before sexual intercourse begins; (2)
when there is immaculate cleanliness of the body and geni-
tals; (3) when it is mutually agreeable to both husband and
wife; and (4) when there is mutually enjoyable physical and
emotional fulfillment.

Couples should realize that oral sex can easily become
habit forming. Also it definitely limits the amount of loving

verbal communication that husband and wife can have during their sex experience.

Many couples inquire if oral sex is not a form of homosexuality. The answer is no. *Homo* refers to sexual activity between members of the same sex, male with male, and female with female. While oral sex is practiced by homosexuals, that alone does not invalidate it for use by husbands and wives. Such line of reasoning would also make sexual intercourse between husband and wife unacceptable because of promiscuity between unmarrieds.

Myth 15

Homosexuality is a socially acceptable form of marriage. As already stated homosexuals are persons who choose to have intimate sex relationships with members of the same sex. Female homosexuals are called *lesbians.* Christianity does not reject homosexuals as persons. We accept them as persons created in the image of God. They have the same social, mental, and spiritual potential as all other people. God loves them. All Christians should love them as persons. We should have a sympathetic and compassionate attitude toward them in their dilemma and do what we can to help them overcome such abnormal behavior. We do not reject homosexuals as persons. We reject their patterns of behavior and their way of life.

Why does Christianity reject the homosexual way of life?

1. Homosexuality is unnatural. Two men do not possess the natural biological equipment for sexual fulfillment. At best it is highly irregular, abnormal, crude, sinful, and falls far short of meeting emotional and spiritual human needs. Paul Popenoe says in *Family Life*, "It deprives the individual of the fullest satisfaction of his inborn nature."

2. Homosexuality is openly opposed and condemned by biblical writings. "You shall not lie with a man as with a woman; it is an abomination" (Leviticus 18:22). Paul, in discussing pagan homosexuals, says,

> So God let them go ahead into every sort of sex sin, and do whatever they wanted to . . . vile and sinful things with each other's bodies. Instead of believing what they knew was the truth about God, they deliberately chose to believe lies . . . their women turned against God's natural plan for them, and indulged in sex sin with each other. And men, instead of having a normal sex relationship with women, burned with lust for each other, men doing shameful things with other men . . . when they gave God up and would not even acknowledge Him, God gave them up to doing everything their evil minds could think of . . . . They were fully aware of God's death penalty for these crimes, yet they went right ahead and did them anyway; and encouraged others to do them, too.
>
> Romans 1:24–28, 32 LB

Paul said to the Corinthians ". . . Don't fool yourselves. Those who live immoral lives, who are idol worshipers, adulterers or homosexuals—will have no share in his kingdom . . ." (1 Corinthians 6:9, 10 LB).

We should beware of some pseudoevangelicals who write books and speak at youth conferences. They are critical of Christianity's approach to homosexuality. They accuse Christianity of being largely responsible for homosexuals. They seldom quote the Bible passages calling homosexuality evil. They never refer to it as being *sinful*. They describe homosexuality in such language as "social maladjustment, emotional immaturity, mental insecurity, and sexual dysfunction."

Suppose we say that there is a small part-truth to the idea that the group structure of society and even organized Christianity are somewhat responsible for causing some people to become homosexuals. This we believe. But the rest of the truth is that each individual homosexual knew that it was wrong, displeasing to God and society, and yet he or she willfully went ahead and adopted homosexual behavior and encouraged others to do so. Therefore each is responsible before God. Society does not mechanically make people become homosexuals against their wills. Each homosexual is a free, active person and is responsible for his individual activities and behavior. All nonhomosexuals live in the same society, and thousands have lived in the same environment and family situation and did not become homosexuals. Why? Because they willfully chose to follow right and reject wrong. Make no mistakes about it, God as the author of the Bible who states truth without mixture of error, condemns homosexuality as a way of life. This we believe.

3. Homosexuality destroys cultures. It (and related excesses, to the neglect of family life) was one of the causes that sent the proud nations of ancient Greece and Rome passing into the pages of history. The Romans learned homosexuality from the Greeks and "outgreeked" the Greeks. Many of the Roman emperors are considered by historians to have been homosexuals. It was this Roman practice that the Bible condemns.

4. If homosexuality was universalized, it would soon depopulate the earth.

5. Homosexuality is often a very impersonal relationship. Homosexuals may have a single affair without knowing anything about the other, not even each other's name, and may never see each other again. Physical release is the only concern. Many homosexuals are constantly looking for new prospects among nonhomosexuals.

6. Instead of being the nice, socially minded, kind, gentle,

happy people that they are often described as being. Dr. Daniel Cappon, Canadian psychiatrist, states that "The natural history of the homosexual person seems to be one of frigidity, impotence, broken personal relationships, psychosomatic disorders, alcoholism, paranoid psychosis (i.e., the mental illness of suspicion and persecution) and suicide." [27] To use the term *gay* to refer to them defies reality.

7. Homosexuality is a leading conveyor of venereal disease. The Associated Press from London, June 12, 1972, quoted Dr. R. D. Catterall, Head of the Middlesex Hospital's Venereal Disease Department as saying:

> In some large cities such as London, New York, Copenhagen, and Paris, more than half of the infectious syphilis seen in hospitals is occurring in homosexual men, many of whom are quite young. Homosexual men tend to be very promiscuous and change their sexual partners frequently . . . today homosexual men form a group which has one of the highest incidences of sexually-transmitted diseases in the world.[28]

8. Old age presents a major problem for homosexuals. They have little or no money, and few friends. They must look to society for food and shelter. They are lonely, depressed, cynical, and exhibit cold contempt for human behavior and life.

We realize that we are treading on thin ice by discussing many of the above mentioned subjects that have been taboo in Christian circles far too long. However, we have the conviction that we have the Christian obligation to tackle these delicate problems in light of scientific research and basic biblical teachings in the hope it will give needed guidance to many fine Christian couples who face these problems.

21

The Pros and Cons of Birth Control

As a social practice, birth control is as old as civilization; as a social movement it is rather new. Contraceptive knowledge in some form, often including magic, has existed for ages. Long before the dawn of written history, primitive peoples made some attempt to adjust their populations to their food supplies. They did this by such cruel methods as the killing of infants, killing of the aged, abortions, and wars. In recent history, birth control has developed into a social movement. Scientific preventive measures have been filtered down to all classes in society. We are now better able to distinguish between rational and irrational, and reliable and unreliable methods of birth control.

The Creator's Plan

As stated in chapter 16 it is generally agreed that the Creator planned two functions for sex life in marriage, namely, (1) sex for a procreative function and (2) for a unitive function, *i.e.*, the one-flesh pleasure of love expression between husband and wife; when the unitive function for love expression is experienced, there is always the possibility of pregnancy, and thus a problem arises. If no effort is made to prevent conception, and if a healthy couple has a regular, normal sex life as the Creator planned for them, there would be one pregnancy after another. Twenty-five children in one family would not be impossible. This is unthinkable. Also it is unthinkable and unchristian for husband and wife to refrain from sex life except for the purpose of reproduction. Therefore, just as man used his mind to invent a hoe to keep weeds out of the corn, so it is necessary for him to use his mind to make certain that the two God-created functions of sex in marriage be allowed to operate without abusing or destroying the people involved in the marriage.

No Biblical Stand

The modern birth control movement is simply a human effort to allow both of these God-created sex functions to operate normally. The Bible gives us no positive or negative statement on birth control. Thus, it is necessary to fall back on broad basic biblical principles to decide the issue. We need to remember that the stern negative demands of the Bible against the abuse of sex was not to say that sex was evil, but rather they were prohibitions to discourage the people of God from joining in the evil sexual practices of the surrounding nations.

Arguments Against

Generally speaking, the arguments opposing birth control have been religious, cultural, and political. Some of the arguments that have been advanced in the past to oppose it are: that it would lead to race suicide; that it is contrary to the welfare of the state; that it is selfishness which tends to promote childless marriages; that it encourages immorality; that it is injurious to health; that it leads to mental disorders; and last—but not least—that it is a violation of nature and the laws of God. Those favoring birth control answer this last argument by saying that birth control is no more against the laws of nature and God than is trimming fingernails, trimming our hair, using medical anesthesia, immunization against disease, control of infection, or any other similar health or medical practice.

Arguments For

Those who advocate birth control argue that it would improve national health conditions in many ways. We would have healthier babies, healthier mothers, and healthier families; we would have a better balance of the population and its resources. It would tend to wipe out poverty through better income of both labor and management; it would reduce the number of ghetto families, and the need for social welfare would decline; it would decrease the number of unwanted, unloved, neglected babies; it would increase education and life fulfillment of young people. It would reduce the need for abortion, and infanticide; it is not a violation of biblical instructions; and last—but not least— it would reduce the fear of pregnancy and make possible better mental-emotional-spiritual relationships between husband and wife through regular and efficient one-flesh love expressions.

This would promote human dignity, enhance the sacredness of human life, exalt motherhood and fatherhood, stabilize family life, and result in moral and social community organization. It needs to be said that those who favor birth control do not oppose the birth of children. They oppose too many children, who cannot be given a normal chance at health, growth, and self-fulfillment. Overpopulation may disturb a healthy balance of world population and natural resources.

It needs to be said that those who led in the birth control movement were not men, medical doctors, or scientists wearing the halo of objectivity. They were determined women, many of them nurses, who were sick of the misery, unhappiness, the disease and squalor in urban ghettos because of too many children born to families in poverty. (Readers, go to your library and read the story of the life of Margaret Sanger.)

Under a system of Christian equality, husband and wife, if possible, ought to agree on the type of contraceptives used. In cases where they do not agree, we recommend that the wife be given veto power over the kind of contraceptives used, since she is the one who becomes pregnant and has the baby. (See *Sexual Happiness in Marriage* for a detailed discussion of planned parenthood through the use of contraceptives.) [29]

22

The Myth of Female Frigidity

A married woman who has not experienced sexual orgasms wants to know *why* she has not and *what* to do in order to achieve normal sexual adjustment. Let us examine this *why* and *what* as well as the meaning of the term *frigidity* as applied to women. Some who refer to a woman as being "frigid" simply mean that she has an aversion to sexual intercourse; but, technically, it is more specific and should be applied to women who cannot reach orgasm during sex relations and therefore do not respond sexually.

Actually there is no such thing as *female frigidity*. Marriage counselors would like to throw this concept in the wastebasket and leave it there. Given time and good sex education, all women who are normal, physically and emotionally, can learn to achieve regular sexual fulfillment in marriage.

The Why of Frigidity

Why do some women appear to be frigid? Some have been taught, directly and indirectly, that "sex is evil," except for reproduction. This idea is a myth! It is unscientific and unchristian! As stated previously, a woman who thinks sex is evil cannot have normal sex life in marriage. Some young women go into marriage who are simply uneducated about sex. They know little or nothing about their own sexual nature, and their young husbands know even less about female sexuality. Under these circumstances, the wife simply does not experience normal sex expression, but she is not frigid.

Another possible reason for so-called frigidity may be poor health, such as being anemic or having other similar health problems or diseases. Fear of an unwanted pregnancy can be a major cause of poor sexual adjustments in marriage. Guilt feelings resulting from a premarriage sex affair or infidelity after marriage may block adjustment. An attempted rape or some unfortunate experience in childhood related to sex may have lingered in a girl's mind across the years, and she fears marriage, men, and sex. An unfaithful husband can become a major road block to his wife's successful adjustment. Some women feel that they are undersexed because their sex drive is not manifested just like that of men. Others feel undersexed because of reading exaggerated imaginary stories written about so-called sexy women in pulp magazines.

Solving the Problem

What can a wife do in order to have pleasurable sexual experiences with her husband? A wife who is unhappy about her sex experience in marriage should talk it over with her husband. The problem may be poor technique on the part of an uneducated, awkward, but well-meaning husband. Most husbands are pleased, happy, and eager to cooperate with their wives. In this search for success there must be frank two-way communication. Both must be guided by positive feelings of love, patience, understanding, and tenderness. They must help each other to feel accepted and to have self-confidence. It often takes time to achieve a good sexual relationship, especially if the bride is in her teens. Relaxed persistence toward the goal pays off, and delay may increase the problem. A couple should be content to learn a little at a time. Success depends equally on the full cooperation of both husband and wife. Success is certain for those who maturely continue the search for it.

A couple may need some outside help. We recommend that they secure a copy of *Sexual Happiness in Marriage* and read and discuss it together. If a wife would prefer a book written by a woman, we recommend any of the several books written by women listed in the bibliography at the end of this book. One can probably find a copy of one of them in the local public library or in your church library.

If neither discussion nor reading a book brings success, the next step would be for the wife to visit her family physician to find out if the problem could be physical. This is especially true if the marriage relationship is physically painful. A wife may prefer to visit a woman gynecologist. In most cases the problem is not physical, but it is well for this fact to be established. Only a doctor can do this.

If a doctor indicates the problem is not physical, the couple should then visit a competent marriage counselor. The couple's pastor or some other pastor may be a qualified marriage counselor. There may be a qualified counselor on the staff of the County Social Welfare Department or the Mental Health Clinic. (See suggestions on finding a marriage counselor in chapter 15.)

Mutually enjoyable sexual experiences in marriage is the focal point of love expression between husband and wife. It tends to relieve anxiety, lessen guilt, and prevent the formation of conflict, tension, and hostility. Unquestionably it is an experience that gives both personal security and inner spiritual poise.

23

The Causes of Male Impotence

One question that all marriage counselors are frequently asked in private conferences is "What causes male impotence?" This is another one of those delicate subjects that has been swept under the rug far too long. It calls for frank, candid answers, which are expressions of truth, sincerity, and honesty—even if the answer offers unwelcome opinion or criticism to those who ask the question.

Definition

Impotence is the inability of a husband to become aroused sexually, to have an erection, to insert the penis in the vagina, and to have an orgasm. *Primary impotence* occurs when a man has never been able to experience sexual intercourse due to some physical deficiency. There are very, very few such cases. *Secondary impotence* occurs when a man has had normal sex experiences and then, for some reason, is not able to have normal sexual experiences.

Many and Varied Reasons

There are many and varied mental, emotional, and physical reasons for impotence. Fear and insecurity may cause impotence. If a husband has had several episodes of failure, the fear that he will fail again may cause him to withdraw from sex, and falsely assume that his sex life is gone forever. A man may have a strong sense of guilt about secret love affairs, past or present, that may cause him to experience some impotence.

Excessive anger, hostility, excitement, or worry may cause male impotence. Some husbands may have lost interest in sex with their wives because of their wives' decline in physical attractiveness, due to aging. A man's mind, his knowledge, his attitudes toward himself and his wife are very important. After age fifty, the source of a man's sex problems is above his shoulders—mental and emotional.

If a man who has been well off financially has major financial reverses, this may cause some impotence. Long years of emotional stress due to conflict, quarreling, and frustration between husband and wife often cause male impotence.

Recommended Scriptures

Some men who think (falsely) that Christianity teaches that sex is evil, or that it is only for reproduction, may become impotent. I recommend that such men read the following passages: Genesis 1:27, 28, 31; 2:24, 25; Proverbs 5:1–19; Song of Solomon 2:3; 8:3; 1 Corinthians 7:2–5; 1 Thessalonians 4:1–8; and Hebrews 13:4.

A wife's increased sexual interest after menopause (partially explained by no more danger of pregnancy and less family responsibility after her children have moved away) may frighten her husband and cause him to feel he is not equal to meeting her sexual needs, and thereby cause impotence. A lack of education and knowledge concerning a man's sexual nature may cause impotence. A male's ego and his sex ability are tied together with iron chains. A man's lack of education concerning the gradual sex decline in the process of aging causes him to lose self-esteem; panic and impotence often follow.

Simple Fatigue

A major cause of impotence is simply fatigue. A man comes home exhausted from a long, hard day's work, and he simply does not have the energy available for a normal sex relationship. Sometimes a couple spends an evening of boring social life, frantically searching for entertainment outside of the home. This leaves them drained and frustrated at midnight. Or some couples waste hours in front of the television watching moronic and inhuman television antics and are exhausted at bedtime.

Fatigue caused by years of formal, mechanical, monotonous, stereotyped routine in life without rest, vacation, variety, or change, may bring on impotence. A lack of communication may cause impotence. Often conflict between husband and wife blocks communication. Free communication between husband and wife about their sexual feelings, attitudes, and needs is a *must* for a continued sex life. A continued loss of sleep may dull sex life and lead to impotence.

Alcohol, Obesity, and Medication

Another cause of impotence is the use of alcohol. Ed Wheat, M.D., says:

> The intake of alcohol does provoke some sexual desire, but it takes away much of the ability to perform or enjoy sexual union. Because alcohol acts as a depressant on the neurological system, it can inhibit a person's sexual functioning as much as it does his coordination or speech. The person who is an alcoholic (defined as one who has lost control of his drinking) almost never has normal sexual ability. Ninety percent of the alcoholics who have developed cirrhosis of the liver are impotent.[30]

Obesity in the husband (or wife, or both) may drain away much of the strength and the desire for intercourse. Obesity lowers our self-image and self-confidence and blocks the mental and emotional imaginative factors necessary for efficient lovemaking. Impotence may be caused by taking certain blood pressure medication, tranquilizers, or illegal narcotics and stimulants now available in our drug culture. Finally, long years of excessive smoking may cause a decline in sexual ability.

We can sum up this discussion by saying that male impotence may develop from fear, sexual excesses, lack of sex education, a twisted set of moral values, or increased age, and is frequently found among those with immature and insecure personalities.

24

Free Love and Open Marriage

Charles and Norma Walker want no children. They have an arrangement they call marriage freedom, in which each should feel free to go out on dates with other members of the opposite sex, and they both do so freely. Sometimes they swap with another couple, sometimes they go out individually. Norma says, "I like to associate with other men. When my husband and I gave each other this freedom, it made us more faithful to each other."

When asked what she meant by "faithful" Norma replied, "We love and trust each other, and do not have the conflicts and problems as in traditional marriages. We do not consider it immoral or sinful. We believe in pleasure for pleasure's sake. The future form of marriage will be like ours. We call it 'social hedonism.' "

The arrangement Norma describes rests upon several phony ideas.

Ten Misconceptions

1. In the first place, she ignores the simple Bible teachings about fidelity in marriage. In the Old Testament, the Seventh Commandment thunders from the mountaintop, *Thou shalt not commit adultery.* As already stated, adultery refers to sexual intercourse by any man or woman, married or single, with a married person who is not his or her spouse. Adultery must involve an unfaithful married person. However, both the married person and the cooperating partner in the act are said to be

guilty of adultery. The word *adultery* is used figuratively to refer to the sinfulness of wicked Israel and other nations, or to individual persons who are unfaithful to God.

Jesus broadened the meaning of adultery by stating that "Whosoever looketh on a woman to lust after her hath committed adultery with her already in his heart" (Matthew 5:28 KJV). In other words, adultery may be an act or an inward condition of the heart in the form of lustful looks and fantasy. An inward motive in the heart often leads to the physical act. Jesus objected to both. In several lists of sins, Paul lists adultery along with (and equal to) such sins as hate, lying, idolatry, stealing, drunkenness, homosexuality, and murder. He concludes that "they which do such things should not inherit the kingdom of God" (*see* 1 Corinthians 5:11; 6:9; Galatians 5:19; Ephesians 5:3; Colossians 3:5). The Bible uses sexual fidelity in marriage as a figure of speech to describe personal faithfulness to God. It uses adultery as a figure of speech to refer to personal unfaithfulness to God. These figures of speech reflect and reinforce the biblical concept of the sacred and divine nature of the institutions of marriage (Hebrews 13:4; James 4:4).

2. The concept of free love and open marriage reveals that Norma and her husband are two very selfish, self-centered people who are interested in their own present desires in disregard for other people. Of course they do not admit their selfishness, nor do they admit that they are antisocial.

3. They assume that "social hedonism" is something *new*. *Hedonism* means "pleasure is the highest good in life." Enlightened people know this idea has been around for centuries (Democritus 460–362 BC, Epicuris 342–270 BC, Jeremy Bentham 1748–1832, John Stuart Mill 1806–1873).

4. Their hedonistic assumption overlooks the fact that the philosophy of pleasure as the highest good is filled with major weaknesses and contradictions such as: (1) one man's pleasure is another man's pain; (2) not all pleasures are of equal worth; (3) some people get pleasure from hate, slander, or sadism; and, (4) pleasure emphasizes *feelings* to the neglect of the will, the intellect, the religious, the social, and the esthetic.

5. Their so-called marriage freedom ignores the inherent relationship between *love* and *jealousy*. The jealousy of an emotionally sick person is to be deplored. Yet, it is normal, natural, and right for an emotionally mature person to be jealous of the husband (or wife) when a third party enters their relationship. In spite of a variety of primitive moral standards, anthropologists believe that marriage jealousy is a universal trait among all peoples. The assumption that trust makes jealousy impossible is out of line with the reality of human nature and the nature of love. Free love is about as strong as a soap bubble, and sooner or later (generally sooner) it will burst into moral bankruptcy.

6. Free love, or "open marriage" as it is being called today, assumes that all traditional marriages are unhappy. This idea holds traditional marriage in scorn and contempt. Yet, sociological research indicates that a large majority of married couples in the USA say that they are "happy" or "very happy." Marriage happiness seldom makes news, but marriage infidelity is a choice morsel of journalistic gossip.

7. Free-love marriage neglects the normal role of children in marriage and reflects the unreasonableness of confused and twisted minds.

8. The assumptions that free love and open marriage will be the style of marriage in the future is naive. Universal application of such an arrangement would have dire consequences in society as a whole. We cannot afford

to ignore the reality of the flow, the stability, and the durability of God's creation in nature.

9. Free love tends to ignore both the past and the future, and it tends to selfishly emphasize the *here* and *now*. It is childish like the phrase "I want what I want when I want it."

10. While pleasure is *good,* it is not an "end in itself." Pleasure is not an act. It results from an attitude or state of mind within a person. Harold H. Titus states that pleasure results from (1) achieving success in a worthwhile work; (2) loyalty and devotion to something greater than one's self; (3) an expanding and friendly interest in other persons; and (4) the cultivation of strong character and a rich inner life. He concludes that "the satisfactions and development of the mind and spirit are higher and more worthy than the pleasures of the body, no matter how intense the latter are." [31]

The Importance of Commitment

I fear that Norma and her husband are caught in a revolutionary trap—a blind alley—that leads eventually to individual disillusionment, failure, despair, and social depersonalization. Their clandestine relationships outside of marriage tend to be formal, mechanical, and physical, and not warm, intimate, personal, love relationships. Free love or open marriage is a bold and contemptuous form of institutionalized adultery. Even Masters and Johnson whose observations of the sex relationship are based on scientific research agree that *commitment* is the key to sexual happiness. [32]

Those who point out that open marriage advocates equality overlook the ten phony ideas that are inherent in free love and open marriage. If husband-wife equality in marriage is to succeed, sexual equality must operate within general biblical guidelines.

25

Sex Life After Sixty

Robert and Blanche Lawson were in their fifties, in the so-called empty-nest period. Mrs. Lawson went to see a marriage counselor privately about their marriage problems. She said that her husband, at fifty-three, had been impotent for the past year. He had refused to seek medical advice. He insisted that his problem was just his age. Mrs. Lawson stated that she felt cheated, frustrated, and unloved. She said that sex was not everything but that it was still very important to her at age fifty-one. She asked, "Is it normal for a fifty-three old, healthy male to be impotent? Am I foolish to insist that he visit a doctor? What can a wife do if her aging husband is impotent?"

Mrs. Lawson's problem is relevant, serious, and critical. *It is a very common problem!* We would assume that a large majority of couples in their middle and late fifties and beyond are disturbed in varying degrees by sex problems.

When Does the Sex Drive Cease?

In reply to her question "Does the sexual activity of a healthy male normally cease at age fifty?" the answer is an emphatic *no!* As stated in chapter 20 our culture is plagued by several major sexual myths. The myth that human sexual life should cease to operate at age fifty or sixty is one of the most evil and damaging—socially, spiritually, emotionally, and physically. It may be the leading ingredient in our sick culture's treatment of its aging populations. This myth—without rhyme or reason—announced dogmatically that at the mystical age of fifty to sixty, a magical iron curtain drops in a person's life, and sex is no more. This idea is not only false, but it is unscientific, irrational, and unchristian. To ask how long does sex last is like asking, "How long does the human heart or lungs last?" Our Creator-God created sex as a part of our total person, and, other things being equal, it can operate parallel with the level of health and functioning of the rest of the body.

What are the facts? There is a gradual slowing down of the male sexual potential as life moves on, just as there is in the strength of the heart and lungs. The body processes do slow down, but this does not mean that they stop. The sexual slowing down in the aging male involves a longer time in achieving erection, full arousal, and less frequent orgasms. This is normal.

The problem that troubles and panics men is the decline in the frequency of orgasms. The myth that sex ends at sixty thrives on the false belief that sexual capacity is identified with the number or frequency of orgasms. In other words, many aging men feel that they must have an orgasm every time they have sexual intercourse. If they do not, they brand themselves as failures. They are often over-whelmed by fright, unreasoning worry, anxiety, and fear, and conclude that they are not only impotent, but that sex is gone forever. Also, their wives often feel that they must succeed in bringing their husbands to orgasm at every attempt, or they are failures as wives. Both ideas are absolutely false.

Whereas a healthy man from age twenty to forty may need and experience orgasm twice a week or more often, a healthy man sixty and beyond may be able to experience orgasm only once per week or twice per month, or less often. This is normal for older men. Those older men who are not familiar with this decline—or who refuse to accept it—often anxiously attempt a sexual orgasm frequently to bolster their ego and self-esteem. This helpless attempt to force erection and orgasm only makes bad matters worse. Sometimes the husband will accuse his wife of being cold and frigid, and may rush out and have an affair with a young woman to prove that he is still a man.

Sex and Orgasms

When a husband has failed to achieve orgasm one or more times, he may withdraw from sex, rather than suffer the experience of failing again, or he may refuse to go to a doctor (or marriage counselor) or both. The results of such action are sad indeed. If a man, age sixty, whose golf average is ninety, has a game with a one hundred and five score, this does not mean that he can never make a score of ninety again. Sex is not something which is there one week and is gone forever the next. To identify sex with the number of orgasms is like identifying baseball with the hit that drives in the winning run. Although the hit that drives in the winning run is certainly a significant part of baseball, the game involves much, much more, such as planning, training, drills, scrimmages, and official games with several innings of play before the hit that drives in the winning run. All of the innings of baseball are normally a pleasurable experience, not just the one hit that wins the game.

In a similiar manner, to equate sex with orgasms overlooks the total nature of sex. Sex is a total continuing experience—one that is involved with the whole of husband-wife relationships. Sex is touching, hugging. Sex is kissing, patting, stroking. Sex is caressing, fondling. Sex is exploration and adventure. Sex is walking, talking, communicating. Sex is playing and having fun. Sex is intimacy and tenderness that is physical, emotional, and spiritual. All of these are sexual experiences, involving pleasure at various levels. Christian love and personal commitment between husband and wife are the ground, the foundation, and the cornerstone of sexual adequacy, and not the number of orgasms.

Sex Without Orgasms

In spite of the fact that there is a gradual slowing down of the male sex drive with age, the sex potential does not stop. A husband in his fifties, sixties, and past, can have an erection and pleasurable sexual intercourse for rather long periods without experiencing an orgasm. He does not need to worry about orgasms. This gives his wife pleasure and time enough to become aroused toward orgasm. The experience can end without either the husband or wife having an orgasm without any damaging results to either.

These experiences are highly pleasurable and satisfying to both husband and wife. They can often repeat such experiences one or more times without orgasm. Therefore, the matter of experiencing sexual release through orgasm is left up to the individual husband and the individual wife. When either husband or wife needs and wants to go on to orgasm in any of their sex experiences, they can do so. There may be occasions when only the husband will be ready for orgasm. This is normal, good, and in line with meaning of 1 Corinthians 7:2–5. On other occasions, both may need and be ready for orgasms. Thus when either wants and needs to go on to orgasm in any of their experiences, they can do so.

How Long Does Sex Last?

Solid research indicates that healthy husbands and wives can enjoy a pleasant sexual experience one or two times per week, well into their eighties. The ability of husband and wife to have regular and pleasurable sexual intercourse for a given period of time without having to worry about orgasm is a blessing the Creator-God added to the sex life of aging couples that compensates for the gradual lengthening of orgastic frequency.

How long does sex last? It is a part of human life. It is a significant and complex part of the mental, emotional, spiritual, and physical nature of man and woman. Some have equated sex with life. They have said that sex is the *highest* good in human life. Some have said that sex is the *only* good in life. This philosophy is irrational and is blind to the total realities of life and must be rejected by thinking Christians. In rejecting the hedonistic (that pleasure is the highest good) concept of sex, it is all too easy for us to rush to the other extreme and embrace the doctrine that sex is evil, especially after sixty. This, too, is irrational and blind to the total realities of human nature. It must be rejected by thinking Christians.

Often when the sex life of a couple ceases at sixty or before, the reason is that husband and wife are in basic emotional conflict over childish common trifles fed by immaturity, insecurity, selfishness, stubbornness, lack of information, or just plain unadulterated sinfulness. We must be realistic. When husband and wife are committed to each other in full Christian love in its broad sense, marriage is first, last, and always a sexual relationship between husband and wife.

What Can a Wife Do If Her Aging Husband Is Impotent?

A wife whose husband is impotent will feel cheated, frustrated, and probably unloved by her husband because of his impotence. She must remember that impotence at fifty or sixty is abnormal. She must realize that the cause of impotence is probably a combination of many problems. She needs to understand that she is the *key* to helping him solve this problem that is embarrassing to both of them.

Now, what can she do? She may be sure that her husband is frightened and depressed! No normal man gives up his sexuality without an inner struggle. She should not blame him. She must not fuss and nag at him, hoping to get him to change. She may assume that both she and her husband are partly responsible for his present impotence. But this is no time for her to blame or to accuse him. He needs help *now*. He needs information, understanding, and empathy. He needs positive love and tenderness.

A Complete Physical Examination

It would be best for an impotent husband to have a thorough physical examination. For the doctor to pronounce him in good health would remove the possibility that his problem may be health. It would give him a ray of hope. His wife should attempt to gradually open lines of communication with her husband. She could read the first part of this chapter to him and help him to realize that his sex life can be renewed and restored. If possible, husband and wife should take a brief vacation, maybe to the mountains or the seashore, and get away from the usual formal grind of life within the four walls of their home. A change of scenery is often helpful.

Questionnaire for Wives

A wife should review and study thoroughly her own attitudes and patterns of behavior toward their past life, including their sex life. She should honestly face the facts concerning such questions as, "Have I had a 'take-it-or-leave-it' attitude toward sex?" "Have I given sex a low priority-rating?" "Am I as attractive as I can be at bedtime?" "Have I denied his approach when he was in definite need?" "Have I been a domineering, overbearing, tyrant-kind of wife?" "Have I tried to help him build up his self-confidence?" "Have I tried to help him get rid of his self-doubt?" "Have I put first such things as making a perfect grocery list, keeping the flowers in a vase well watered, enjoying my 'hobby' and thus neglected my 'hubby'?" "Have I belittled his business and social problems?" "Have I been a companion and tried to listen and understand him and his point of view?"

An impotent husband is in need of help. His wife is in the best position to give him the help that he needs. A good sex life does not start in the bedroom at 11:30 P.M., tacked onto the tired tag end of a frustrating day.

A wife should gently, tactfully, and prayerfully take the

initiative in an attempt to restore a pleasant sex life in their marriage. She has much going for her. The facts are on her side. Assuming she is past menopause, she does not have to contend with using contraceptives. Hence she has the advantage of relaxed expressions of love and spontaneity.

Two-way Communication

However, there may be some major problems in a marriage relationship that is blocking good sex life. Something has shattered the husband's self-confidence. Only husband and wife together can restore it. Under these circumstances, one would assume communication between a wife and husband is at a very low ebb, probably nil. In order to break out of this sexual impasse, the wife should initiate two-way communication on the subject of sex life. They should have some long, quiet, calm talks together, several of them. A wife should verbalize her feelings and attitudes, and allow her husband to do the same. If necessary, write them out and read them together.

Couples must bring their problems out in the open and see them objectively and in reality for what they are. They should agree on a course of action designed gradually to restore normal sex life. Both husband and wife must be equally concerned and equally aggressive in attempts to get back to normal sex life. A wife should take more initiative than in the past. It is possible for the two of them together to work out their problems to the satisfaction of both. If a couple find they cannot, they should seek help from a qualified marriage counselor who will keep their problem in professional confidence. (*See* chapter 15.)

Under normal circumstances God did not expect sex life in marriage to end at fifty or sixty. The Bible calls for sexual happiness *in marriage*. It insists that the husband should regularly meet his wife's sexual needs, and the wife should regularly meet her husband's sexual needs (1 Corinthians 7:3). No man (or woman) wants sex life to end at sixty.

26

How to Keep Romance in Marriage

During a church sponsored Marriage and Family Life Conference, the leader of a husband and wife seminar chided the couples about neglecting one another. Then he pressed the idea that husband and wife should continue to be "romantic" after marriage.

After the seminar, a Mrs. Shipley kidded him about his use of the word *romance*. In substance, she said, "I even question the genuineness of premarriage romance. Therefore, isn't it rather normal for so-called romantic relationships to cool off and become routine after marriage? We have been married ten years, and have two children. We have a good marriage. We love each other. We trust each other. We take each other for granted. Our life-style follows rather established procedures. Honestly now, aren't you being rather unrealistic in talking so enthusiastically about romance in marriage?"

Frankly, I am suspicious of Mrs. Shipley's description of the love life between her and her husband. When a husband-wife's love cools off, becomes routine, and they take each other for granted, they are drifting toward certain conflict, unhappiness, and a possible divorce. Certainly they are missing the tender, intimate, personal relationships that belong to married love. Husband and wife have to work at the process of married love in order to enjoy the normal fruits of romantic happiness.

Romance: A Definition

A definition of romance is in order. David Mace has popularized a definition of what he calls "bogus romance" in three steps. *Step One:* A dashing handsome young boy meets a beautiful young girl. Both are suddenly gripped with a strange feeling they identify as love at first sight. *Step Two:* Both immediately leave everything and everybody for this new-found, irresistible feeling. They get married. *Step Three:* Six months later this strange new feeling that had come so quickly has just as suddenly and strangely gone. They secure a divorce and start over. This is a rather accurate description of romance as described in movies, television, slick magazines, and cheap paperback love stories. This type of romantic love is characterized by physical passion, lust, wild imagination, excessive enthusiasm, and mystery. It is an expression of a sick emotional and mental disorder. It is a deep and intense case of neurotic stupidity. It is not love. It is counterfeit romance.

A more reasonable description of premarriage romance might be described as follows: A boy and girl meet through friends in a social situation. They are attracted to each other physically; she appears beautiful and he appears handsome. They get acquainted, associate with each other, find they have many values, ideals, and goals in common; gradually over weeks and months, love develops, which is characterized by mutual physical attraction and a mutual feeling of concern, tenderness, and affection for one another. The well-being of one another matters more than their own well-being. This is premarriage love. It is premarriage romance. This process is normal, intelligent, mature, and Christian. *Romance* is simply the process of love experience. It is a good word!

Mutual Openness

To keep romance in marriage, husband and wife should practice mutual openness in attitudes, words, and deed.

They should be able to see clearly through each other's feelings and emotions, like seeing a fish in a crystal-clear lake. To close up like a clam does not indicate depth or wisdom, but shallowness, insecurity, and fear. Husband and wife should let their feelings flow outward to each other like the music from a mockingbird, or the flashes of light from her diamond. Some couples can live together for twenty years without knowing each other. This is sad, sad indeed. They are missing the ripe fruits of romantic love. No! Love cannot be taken for granted. Love must be openly manifested. Love can be known and can grow only through free expression.

Some How To's

To keep romance in marriage, show small courtesies to one another. Wait on one another, open doors, give up the easy chair, sew on buttons, carry burdens, serve a cool drink of water, be helpful. Kind deeds stoke the cooling fires of romance into mature, warm, tender expressions.

Husband and wife need to communicate in gentle affectionate words. If the meal was good, say so. Call each other by your pet names. At formal group occasions it may be inappropriate to use these names, but in everyday husband-wife person-to-person home relations, upstairs, downstairs, indoors, outdoors, call each other *Sweetheart* or some other equally complimentary pet name.

Friends

Of course, husband and wife need social friends, close mutual friends. Mature people are friendly to all, but some close, personal, intimate special friendship with other couples will fulfill their social and emotional roles and needs. (However, couples should avoid exclusive relationships with just one couple all the time.) To be completely isolated from society breeds loneliness, self-righteousness, fault-finding, and ugly judgmental attitudes.

Happiness in marriage can never be considered as having been completed. Through the years, age, personal experiences, and social and environmental situations are constantly changing. Therefore, husband and wife must constantly be in the process of change, growth, and progress, both within themselves and toward one another. Yet, they must not forget that there are three major divine eternal principles and life guidelines that do not change, even though persons and culture are constantly changing. Thus husband and wife, on the one hand, must continually relate both to their changing inner realities and the changing realities of their culture; on the other hand, they must relate themselves to the realities of the divine fixed spiritual, moral, and social guiding principles.

Need for Romantic Love

Finally, husband and wife relationships should be dotted with kisses and caresses. A few lazy, hard-hearted, unromantic neurotics may object to this, but we suspect that their homes and hearts are as cold as the North Pole and are as sad as a major disaster scene. One warm kiss and one fond embrace can do more to bring back roses to cheeks and light to the eyes than all the gold in Fort Knox or all the jewels of Jackie Kennedy Onassis and Elizabeth Taylor combined. Embraces and kisses at morning, noon, and night are a cure for a thousand marriage ills. It is as foolish to question the value of tender kisses and embraces as it is to question 220 volts of electricity. Anger manifests itself in fights, and sorrow manifests itself in tears. As sparks fly upward, so love manifests itself in tender kisses and embraces. God created us thus. Thousands of starved hearts are withering away because they have been denied their need to love and be loved romantically by that one special person of the opposite sex.

Love is a gift which God gives us,
A joy both to have and to share—
Love is of earth and of heaven,
Its home can be found anywhere.

How wonderful that when God made us,
He gave us this mystical gift—
Which warmly responds when we give it away,
By returning to give us a lift!

27

Conclusion: Equality Is God's Plan for Us

Man and woman were both created in the image of God. They were both given authority to rule over and utilize the animal and vegetable kingdom. They are equals as sinners before God and in receiving salvation in Christ, God's grace, and eternal life. In the New Testament church both were accepted as believers and were baptized. They are equals in sexual needs and rights. They are social equals in the Christian family and community. No woman can be born without a sperm cell and no man can be born without an egg cell. That is, every woman's existence is dependent upon the union of a *man* and a woman; every man's existence is dependent upon the union of a *woman* and a man. Both owe their existence to God. In agape love, Christian husbands and wives should each consider the needs and rights of the other above their own. They are both "fellow laborers" and "co-workers" in the Lord. The Ten Commandments and the Golden Rule include both men and women. These basic truths indicate husband-wife equality.

Two Guidelines

There are two guidelines that should lead and direct the roles and the interpersonal relationships of husband and wife in the home and in society. They are (1) the basic biblical doctrine of husband-wife equality; and, (2) the biological differences inherent in the male and female. This is the paradox of all paradoxes. The Creator created these differences to complete and fulfill both man and woman, and they in no way repeal or abolish their equality.

No More Power Struggles

Directed by these two guidelines, Christian equality should keep husband and wife from getting locked into insecure, immature, and jealous power struggles. Human nature—frail and sinful as it is—can become spiteful, malicious, and vicious. If one wins, the other loses. Usually neither wins and both lose. Christian equality can unlock dead-center conflict, and both husband and wife can learn to lead, to follow, to talk, to listen, to love, and to be loved. Secrecy is blocked and each other's unsatisfied needs, desires, and feelings are brought out into the open and understood. Two-way communication and psychological support follow, promoting mutual trust and care. They each share their dreams and fantasies about and with each other. Both husband and wife cease tearing each other down and start to lift each other up.

Tension and stress are replaced by relaxation, quiet rest, and understanding, and both learn to change and to grow in the Christian graces. Continued emotional support and intimate closeness can become a number one priority. Each partner will seek to nourish and enrich the life of the other. Their conflicting values will now tend to coincide, agree, and harmonize. Thus problems related to finances, in-laws, child care, social life, and other home and community roles are no longer major problems but are gradually solved by the positive attitudes and feelings that flow from Christian equality.

Christianity and Human Sexuality

As the day follows the night, so spiritual and emotional equality, growth, unity, and happiness will be followed by physical one-flesh unity, and fulfillment. Christianity and human sexuality are close friends, not mortal enemies. The better Christians husbands and wives are, the better they meet each other's sexual needs; the better the sex life they enjoy, the better Christians they ought to be. The love that husbands and wives have for each other is symbolic of Christ's love for His bride, the church, which is exemplified by His death on the cross.

Sexual intercourse is not just a shallow, fleeting, flippant, fly-by-night, casual episode. It is something more than a meeting of two bodies. It is not something that creates love. It expresses and feeds love that already exists. Sexual intercourse in Christian marriage expresses personal pleasure at its highest heights and deepest depths—pleasure that is spiritual, emotional, and physical. At the same time—paradoxically—it is intimate, personal, and sacred. Personal love between husband and wife expressed through sexual intimacy calls for privacy.

God's Plan

God has stated that it is not good for man to be alone. He has ordained that man "leave" his parents, "cleave" to his wife, and "be" one flesh. Truly, Christian equality and agape love guided by basic biblical principles in marriage, can create shared joy, warmth, affection, excitement, humor, fun, loyalty, fidelity, tenderness, intimacy, pure physical pleasure, and spiritual unity. These all flow back and forth, circulate and return between husband and wife in the mature sexual one-flesh fulfillment planned by our Creator-God.

Christian equality is not competitiveness, except in competing to see which can bring greater pleasure, joy, and happiness to the other. Love and submission (doing what pleases the other) are two sides of the same coin. When one spouse, in the traditional sense, considers himself above the other, each tends to live in his own little world. When equality is practiced, both gravitate into one world characterized by a greater depth of intimacy, security, self-confidence, and self-esteem. This provides the soil for both to grow in and blossom through the years.

The nearest place to hell on earth for a husband or wife is in an unhappy, unchristian, bickering, quarreling, fighting home. The nearest place to heaven on earth for a husband or wife is in a happy, peaceful Christian home.

APPENDIX

WHAT DOES THE BIBLE SAY About Husband-Wife Equality?

There are many broad, positive doctrinal statements in the Bible whose inner context and basic thrust unquestionably and authoritatively verify and confirm the doctrine of husband-wife equality. Let us now examine these passages.

The Image and Likeness of God

In Genesis 1:26, 27, we read, "Let us make man [human beings] in our own image, after our likeness . . . . So God created man [human beings] in His own image, in the image of God he created him [human beings]; male and female he created them." (The idea that man and woman both were created in the likeness of God is repeated in Genesis 5:1–2.) This passage in context indicates that men and women are different from, and are superior to the other life (plants and animals) that God has created. Both man and woman were made in the "image" and "likeness" of God.

They have nonphysical qualities like God. That is, they are free within limitations. They have the capacity to think, to choose, to speak, to act. They are self-conscious, have self-knowledge and self-control. They can remember the past, plan the future, hold values, possess motives, and distinguish between true and false, right and wrong, and good and evil. They can choose between alternatives and accept responsibility. They can experience fellowship and interaction with God, other persons, social situations, and the physical environment.

163

In simple language, man and woman are *both* made out of the same kind of "nonphysical stuff" that God is, except human beings are finite (limited) and God is infinite (unlimited). It is rather difficult to pay human beings a higher tribute than this. Thus Genesis 1:26, 27 says unequivocally that male and female are *both* made in the image of God and are *equals* in God's plan of creation.

One Flesh

The biblical teaching of "one flesh" calls for husband-wife equality. In Genesis 2:24, we read, "Therefore a man leaves his father and his mother and cleaves to his wife, and they become one flesh." Note that Jesus (Matthew 19:5, Mark 10:7–8) and Paul (1 Corinthians 6:16) both use this one-flesh concept as taught in Genesis. The term *one flesh* is necessary to our Christian interpretation of husband-wife relationships. One flesh certainly does not mean that the physical body of the husband and the physical body of the wife become one physical body. Nor does it refer to a momentary fly-by-night sexual episode of near-strangers. It is not just a union of the genital organs, although it includes this. Husband and wife cannot have one flesh without sexual intercourse. Derrick Sherwin Bailey states beautifully that the true one flesh

> . . . is effected by intercourse following consent between a man and a woman who love one another and who act freely, deliberately, responsibly, and with the knowledge and approval of the community, and in so doing (whether they know it or not) conform to the Divine Law.[33]

This act is both physical and nonphysical. The two become one yet they remain two individuals. They become one physically in that their bodies are united through their genital organs. It is an equality relationship in that they both have sexual desires and needs. They love one another. They need each other. They are dependent on one another to fulfill their needs. Neither is passive. Both are active. He gives himself to her. She gives herself to him. He becomes aware of his total nature and his wife's total nature. She becomes aware of her total nature and her husband's total nature. This awareness is at the highest, deepest, and broadest possible level of awareness.

One flesh is a total relationship of the whole person of the husband to the total person of his wife, and the whole person of the wife to the total person of her husband. One flesh affects the whole self of both husband and wife. The two become one, yet they remain two separate individuals. Each and every succeeding act of intercourse continues, maintains, and renews the one-flesh unity. This unity is the result of the special creative plan of God for male and female.

It is difficult to imagine how the hierarchy doctrine of husband/dominant-wife/subordinate relationship could make any contribution to this sacred act. Equality, on the other hand, tends to encourage sharing and giving, and thereby, eliminates problems and discord prevalent where one mate is dominant. The one-flesh unity is in direct conflict with the dominant/subordinate concept.

Equal Responsibilities

Genesis 1:28 says, "And God blessed *them* and God said to them [man and woman], 'Be fruitful and multiply, and fill the earth and subdue it; and have dominion over the fish . . . birds . . . and over every living thing that moves upon the earth' " (*italics ours*). Thus, men and women are equals not only in being made in the image of God, but are equals in the responsibilities of populating the earth and in ruling over the rest of created life, such as plants, fish, birds, animals, and every living thing. Therefore, the concept of equality of man and woman in the plan of God is deeply rooted in the account of Creation in the first chapter of Genesis.

Equal in Sinfulness

There are many Scriptures stating that men and women are equal sinners before God by nature and by choice. "For there is not a just man upon earth, that doeth good and sinneth not" (Ecclesiastes 7:20 KJV). "For all have sinned, and come short of the glory of God" (Romans 3:23 KJV). "Everyone dies because all of us are related to Adam, being members of his sinful race, and wherever there is sin, death results . . ." (1 Corinthians 15:22 LB). There is no biblical or scientific evidence that either man or woman is more sinful or more spiritual than the other. They are equals in their sinful nature before God.

Equal Access to God

Martin Luther's emphasis on "justification by faith" flowing from Paul's statement, "Therefore, since we are justified by faith, we have peace with God through our Lord Jesus Christ" (Romans 5:1), has been generally accepted by evangelicals. It is called the doctrine of "the priesthood of the believer." This means that there is no priest or human mediator between man and God. (Every person, male or female, comes directly to God and receives saving grace through repentance and faith.) This direct access to God is taught throughout the New Testament. For example, Paul said to Timothy, "For there is one God, and there is one mediator between God and men, the man Christ Jesus, who gave himself as a ransom for all . . ." (1 Timothy 2:5, 6).

This teaching—the priesthood of the believer—is in direct conflict with the hierarchy teaching of the family. The dominant-subordinate doctrine tends to throttle woman's initiative. She is asked to "keep silent in the church." She is "never to teach men." If she wants to know anything about religion, "Let her ask her husband." This is not to suggest that hierarchy thinkers would have a woman's husband be her priest. However, if the hierarchy teaching was carefully carried out in the lives of women (which it is not), it would certainly present obstacles in her pathway that would interfere with and discourage her from freely taking the initiative to claim her direct access to God.

This is further confirmed by the apostle Peter. He cautions men, "You husbands should try to understand the wives you live with, honouring them as physically weaker yet equally heirs with you of the grace of life . . ." (1 Peter 3:7 PHILLIPS). The superior strength of men does not give a husband a better chance at salvation than his wife. Salvation comes by grace through personal repentance from sin and faith in Christ. The doctrine of the universal priesthood of the believer is further confirmed by the favorite passage of evangelicals—the mountain peak of the Gospel:

> For God so loved the world that he gave his only Son, that whoever believes in him should not perish but have eternal life.
>
> John 3:16

That husbands and wives (men and women) are equals in receiving God's grace in salvation and in eternal life is a universal biblical teaching. Before God, men and women are equals in the plan of redemption in Christ.

Equal in Sexual Relationships

Men and women are equals as husbands and wives in the sacred portals of their intimate, interpersonal sexual relationships. The clearest passage in the New Testament setting forth the basic truths concerning the sexual rights and needs of husband and wife is found in 1 Corinthians 7:2–5. For our purposes it is helpful to give this passage the following free translation:

Because of the strong nature of the sexual drive each man should have his own wife and each woman should have her own husband. The husband should regularly meet his wife's sexual needs, and the wife should regularly meet her husband's sexual needs. In marriage, just as the wife's body belongs to her husband and he rules over it, so in marriage the husband's body belongs to his wife and she rules over it. Do not refuse to meet each other's sexual needs unless you both agree to abstain from intercourse for a short time in order to devote yourselves to prayer. But because of your strong sexual needs, when this short period is past, continue to meet each other's sexual needs by coming together again in sexual intercourse.

In this passage, both husband and wife have definite and equal sexual needs that should be met in marriage. Cheryl's body does not belong to her; it belongs to her husband, Melvin, and he rules over it. Likewise, Melvin's body does not belong to him; it belongs to his wife, Cheryl, and she rules over it. Verse 4 is saying that husband and wife rule over each other's sexuality. It is not the responsibility of the wife to meet her own sexual needs. Rather, it is the husband's responsibility continually to meet his wife's sexual needs, and it is the wife's responsibility continually to meet her husband's sexual needs. It is a *cooperative* experience. In this manner, the total needs of both are met.

The fact that the husband and wife each enjoy meeting each other's sexual needs in this equal unity relationship does not conflict with the Hebrew-Christian concept of a devout spiritual life, such as following fully the will of God, growth in grace, Christian service, and stewardship. Rather, this Scripture implies that a meaningful Christian life and meaningful sexual adjustment in marriage really go together.

This entire passage teaches repeatedly and unequivocally the parallel equality of husband and wife in their sexual needs and rights.

Social Equals

Husbands and wives (men and women) are social equals to one another in the Christian family and community. Paul, in talking to the Ephesians (5:21) about how to live the new life in Christ says, "Keep on living in subordination to one another out of reverence to Christ" (as translated by C. K. Williams in the New Testament in Plain English). Here *subordination* means that all Christians should place the welfare of all persons (whether they are friends or enemies, Christians or non-Christians) above their own self-interest. This includes all men and women, all husbands and wives. Paul said to the Christians at Rome, "Love one another with brotherly affection; outdo one another in showing honor" (Romans 12:10). The second greatest commandment of all, "You shall love your neighbour as yourself" (Matthew 22:39; Galatians 5:14; James 2:8), calls for equality between men and women. Thus, Ephesians 5:21 and many other passages definitely call for social equality between husband and wife.

Equal Heirs

Galatians 3:28 is one of the major biblical cornerstones calling for equality between husband and wife. Paul wrote his letter to the Galatians to defend the Gospel of Christ from the false legalism of the Judaizers. Soon after the conversion of the Galatians, the Jews who had become Christians joined their young congregations and began to preach legalistic doctrines. They insisted that observance of all Jewish law, including circumcision, was necessary for all Christians, Gentiles as well as Jews. Thus Gentiles had to become Jews in order to become Christians. This meant that Christianity, like Judaism, was for Jews only. It was

salvation by works. Paul, in Galatians, refutes them with
the central theme that the Gospel of Christ is a free, universal gospel of grace intended for all men of all races (Galatians 3:26). Paul calls for Christian freedom in terms of
salvation by grace through faith. He calls for Christian freedom from the legalistic Jewish law. In his vigorous defense,
Paul insists that man is not justified by the works of the law,
but through faith in Jesus Christ (Galatians 2:16). He said
further that "in Christ Jesus you are *all* sons of God
through faith" (Galatians 3:26, *italics added*). He is saying
that since believers are united in Christ, there is no place for
discrimination against the Gentiles or any other group of
people. Verse 28, which stands tall out of chapter 3, is
saying that when we put on Christ by grace through faith
there is no room for discrimination. Paul outlines three
groups who are often discriminated against. In simple, positive language he says, "There is neither Jew nor Greek, [all
racial discrimination is rejected], there is neither slave nor
free [all social class discrimination is rejected], there is
neither male nor female [all sex discrimination is rejected];
for you are all one in Christ Jesus" (Galatians 3:28). Discrimination against these group divisions are opposed to
and in conflict with "oneness" and "unity" in Christ.
Therefore this passage is an unequivocal, positive doctrine
stating that male and female (husbands and wives) are
equal heirs.

Paul's Positive Statement on Equality

In 1 Corinthians 11:11–12 Paul makes a positive doctrinal
statement explaining the equal relationship of men and
women. In the first part of the chapter, he is discussing the
traditions used in the churches involving men praying with
their hats on (head covered) and women praying without a
veil on (head uncovered). In Corinth, women prostitutes
went about with their heads uncovered. Some of the women
converts in Corinth, in enjoying their new freedom in

Christ, were coming to worship with heads uncovered. Since they met in private homes in small groups, the new women converts saw no reason why they should wear veils. It may be that some Jewish converts (whose tradition was that women should wear veils in worship) attending these meetings objected. Thus Paul was trying to avoid conflict in the worship services. In an effort to protect women in this specific situation, Paul calls their attention to the practice of the church, and explains the reason for the practice—prostitutes going around with their heads uncovered.

In the midst of his discussion Paul realizes that the Corinthians might be misled to believe his statements to be a universal command for all generations. Therefore he gives a positive doctrinal statement about the equality of men and women. It is a statement in parenthesis designed to avoid such interpretation. He says, "Of course, in the sight of the Lord neither 'man' nor 'woman' has any separate existence. For if woman was made originally from man, no man is now born except by a woman, and both man and woman, like everything else, owe their existence to God" (1 Corinthians 11:11, 12 PHILLIPS). Then Paul continues by saying, "Use your own judgment . . ." which indicates that the local tradition he was discussing was not intended as a universal doctrinally binding statement for all times.

We must not miss the point. Paul is warning all men, who tend to think of themselves as superior to women because they were created before women, that, following Creation, all men are born of women. This tends to turn male pride into reason and to balance the scales in the direction of equality. First Corinthians 11:11, 12 *calls for equality between male and female.*

Humility in Equality

The New Testament teaches that humility is one of the central characteristics of Christian behavior. When the disciples of Jesus asked him, "Who is the greatest in the kingdom of heaven?'' Jesus used a little child as an illustration and answered them, ''Whoever humbles himself like this child, he is the greatest in the kingdom of heaven'' (Matthew 18:1–4). Paul says, ''Do nothing from selfishness or conceit, but in humility count others better than yourselves. Let each of you look not only to his own interests, but also to the interests of others'' (Philippians 2:3, 4).

To demand that the husband be final authority over his wife, and that she submit to his ideas, is in conflict with the Christian concept of humility. It opens to the husband the gate of possible selfishness and vainglory. It puts him in the position of considering himself better than his wife. The New Testament concept of Christian humility rejects the husband/authority-wife/subordinate teaching and calls for husband-wife equality.

Jesus Viewed Women As Equals

The life and teachings of Jesus indicate that He thought of women as equals with men, and that He treated them as equals. If He had thought that women were subordinate members of a human hierarchy, He would surely have stated this concept openly. The patriarchal concept of superior man and inferior woman was fully accepted and practiced by societies of His day, including the Hebrew, Greek, and Roman cultures. The same was true of the cultures of the surrounding nations.

In the New Testament world, women were secluded in their homes and kept in ignorance. It was unthinkable for a woman to be so brazen as to speak in public or to teach men. She could not vote. She could not be educated. She could not own property. She was often a sex object and human breeder. She had to bear the heavy burden of a moral and sexual double standard. A Greek father, who freely enjoyed meeting his physical desires with concubines and prostitutes, could sell his daughter into slavery if she lost her virginity. Divorce was the prerogative of men.

These patriarchal practices constitute one of the darkest pages in human history.

Jesus' family concepts were characterized by belief in strict monogamy (one husband and one wife, permanently). In His life and teachings He attacked head-on the husband/dominant-wife/subordinate practices of His day. Instead of treating women as second-class citizens or inferior slaves, He condemned the arrogance of men, and treated women as persons created in the image of God with value and worth equal to men. Much of Jesus' public ministry was directed toward meeting the needs of women who were neglected and rejected by society. He healed the mother-in-law of Simon Peter (Mark 1:29–31). Although she was considered unclean, He healed the woman with a hemorrhage (Luke 8:43–48). In response to the pleas of Mary and Martha, He raised Lazarus from the dead (John 11:17–44).

He often addressed His teachings to women and used women as illustrations of many spiritual truths. Although it was unthinkable for a Jewish rabbi, Jesus often engaged women in conversation. He had a long conversation with the Samaritan woman at the well of Sychar (John 4:5–30). He was kind to and forgave the woman taken in adultery (John 8:3–11). He did not condone her behavior, but He defended her against the men who were ready to kill her.

Many women, some married and some single, followed Jesus throughout His ministry. Among them were Mary Magdalene, Mary, the mother of James and Joseph, the mother of James and John, Mary and Martha, Joanna (the wife of Herod's steward), Susanna, and many others. The women who followed Jesus were from the upper, middle, and lower classes. Women followed Jesus on His last journey to Jerusalem (Matthew 27:55, 56). Their presence at the crucifixion (Luke 23:49) must have comforted Him. Women prepared spices and ointments for His burial (Luke 23:55, 56). They were first at the tomb on the morning of the Resurrection (Matthew 28:1). They were the first to witness that Jesus was raised from the dead (Luke 24:1–11).

Why did women accept the teachings of Jesus and follow him? He treated them as persons of value and worth, equal to men. Why did Jesus violate openly the male/dominant-female/subordinate teachings of the first century New Testament world? Simply because women are equals with men in the creative plan of God.

Early Christian Women Leaders

It is difficult to understand the hierarchy theory in light of Paul's attitude toward Christian women leaders in the churches. In closing his letter to the Romans, Paul tenderly sent greetings to twenty-nine people. At least one third of them were women. He begins the chapter by saying, "I commend to you our sister Phoebe, a deaconness of the church at Cen-chre-ae" (Romans 16:1). Does this not mean that she was an officer in the church? In Romans 16:3–5, Paul sends greetings to Prisca (Priscilla) and mentions her name before her husband Aquila. Also, in Acts 18:26, when their names are mentioned, Priscilla's name is mentioned before her husband Aquila. This may have been because of her Christian zeal and leadership ability. They were close Christian friends of Paul. Priscilla and Aquila moved their business of tent making from Corinth to Ephesus in order to help Paul start a missionary work there. While Paul was away in Jerusalem, Priscilla and Aquila met Apollos, the converted Jew, and heard him preach. He was a learned man and an eloquent speaker. When they saw that Apollos seemed to know only the baptism of John, Priscilla and Aquila kindly took him aside and "expounded to him the way of God more accurately" (Acts 18:26). Could it be that since her name is stated first, that Priscilla was the leader in this ministry to Apollos? If so, we have Priscilla, a Christian woman, taking the lead in correcting and teaching an outstanding Jewish Christian man.

On two occasions Paul referred to women as "fellow

workers" or "helpers" (KJV) in the Lord (Romans 16:3; Philippians 4:3). It is difficult to harmonize Paul's use of women in his missionary activities with some of the assumed universal teachings of the hierarchy advocates, namely, (1) women must keep silence in church; (2) women must not teach men; and, (3) women must not exercise authority over men. Priscilla was not silent. She taught Apollos more perfectly. She exercised authority over him.

Similar Instructions for those Married to Nonbelievers

The Corinthian church asked Paul a question about how their church should handle the problem of a believer married to an unbeliever. He gives them a detailed reply in 1 Corinthians 7:10–17. It is significant that he gives parallel instructions to both husband and wife. He instructs both the believing wife and the believing husband not to leave their nonbelieving spouse just because he or she is not a Christian (verse 10). If the nonbelieving spouse wants to stay married to the believing husband or wife, do not divorce or leave them (verse 12, 13). He points out that the believing husband or wife may influence the nonbelieving spouse to become a believer (verse 14). He says further that if the believing husband or wife leaves the nonbelieving spouse, the children might not grow up to be believers in such a situation (verse 14). Then he says that if the nonbelieving spouse is eager to divorce or leave either the believing husband or wife, let them go, and in such cases neither the believing husband or wife will be held responsible (verse 15). This is another significant example of how the Holy Scriptures considers men and women to be equals in marriage.

Use of Gifts—Equally

The Scriptures teach that Christians should use their gifts (1 Corinthians 12); talents (Matthew 25:14–30); and bodies (Romans 12:1) in service in the Kingdom of God. We are to grow in grace and knowledge of the Lord Jesus Christ. We are exhorted to develop our minds, natural endowments, and personalities to the maximum in service to Christ. Do these exhortations not refer to both men and women? Due to the emphasis on women's education in our day, these passages are more significant in the lives of women than ever before. Yet the hierarchy doctrine, placing wives in what Lewis B. Smedes calls in *Sex for Christians* the "one down" position, tends to block the Christian growth of wives and therefore their growth in marriage.

It is difficult to keep from concluding that a wife in a husband-authority marriage is often gradually blocked from Christian growth in grace and prevented from functioning in normal husband-wife happiness.

Refuting the Wife-Slave Parallel

There are many Bible passages involving the words *servant, bond servant,* and *slave.* They include the Christian concept of service, which seems to refute the hierarchy theory. Jesus said to His disciples, ". . . whoever would be great among you must be your servant, and whoever would be first among you must be your slave" (Matthew 20:26, 27). Also Jesus said, "You must not be called 'leaders' for you have only one Leader, and that is Christ. Whoever is greatest among you must be your servant. Whoever exalts himself will be humbled, and whoever humbles himself will be exalted" (Matthew 23:10–12, as translated by C. K. Williams). In light of these teachings, it is difficult to understand why some insist that the husband is the "master" or "leader" in the family; that he has the authority to make final decisions; that the wife should be subordinate to him and be secondary authority in the family. The hierarchy theory is simply out of line with Jesus' theory of greatness and service in the Kingdom of God.

Paul K. Jewett [34] and Letha Scanzoni and Nancy Hardesty [35] are correct when they argue that if Ephesians 5:22, 23 teaches the hierarchy theory, it follows that Christians would have to advocate slavery on the same grounds. After Paul said in Ephesians 5:21, "Be subject one to another out of reverence for Christ," he gave three simple illustrations to set forth what he meant by Christians being subject or related one to another. The third illustration (Ephesians 6:5–9) was the slave-master relationship. Slavery was widely practiced in Paul's day in Ephesus and in the surrounding nations. Paul was not condoning the practice of slavery, but was giving an illustration of how Christian slaves were to relate themselves to their masters and other Christians out of reverence for Christ. One of the most ugly spots in the history of American Christianity is that many Christians in both the North and the South in the pre-Civil War days justified slavery on biblical grounds using Ephesians 6:5–9 as authority. In these days no thinking Christians would defend slavery on biblical grounds, and, in fact, not even the hierarchy thinkers would defend it. Yet they argue as pro-slavery Christians did before the Civil War from a parallel passage (Ephesians 5:22, 23) to deny some freedom to wives by making them subordinates to their husbands. In light of the fact that Ephesians 5:21 ties the husband-wife illustration (5:22–23) and the master-slave illustration (6:5–9) together in the same binding parallel relationship, it is puzzling to understand how many otherwise humble and scholarly Christians can interpret them in two different ways by accepting one as universally binding and rejecting the other.

Other Biblical Examples of Equality

The Fifth Commandment "Honor your father and your mother . . ." (Exodus 20:12) seems to place husband and wives on equal levels. Also, the passage often called the Golden Rule "Treat others as you want them to treat you" (Luke 6:31, LB) includes both men and women and assumes equality.

Both men and women were accepted as believers (Acts 5:14) and were baptized (Acts 8:12).

These passages, and many others, seem to leave no room for authoritative husbands or subordinate wives.

WHAT DOES THE BIBLE SAY
About Wife-Submission?

From our study of Ephesians 5 (chapter 2), we have learned that it is easy to read hierarchy doctrines into the Scriptures. Also it is easy to form a quick conclusion about a passage without considering the context of the passage and its relationship to the basic principles of the Scriptures. These lessons learned from Ephesians 5 will help us in understanding other problem passages, such as: 1 Corinthians 11:5; 14:34; Colossians 3:18, 19; 1 Timothy 2:9–11; Titus 2:5; and 1 Peter 3:1–4. It is easy to fall into the trap of reading wife-submission into these passages.

We now turn our attention to an examination of these passages. Does Paul believe in the husband/authority-wife/submissive doctrine? If so, does he insist it is a universal mandate for all time? We will discuss four topics involved in these passages as follows: (1) woman's dress in public; (2) woman's silence in worship services; (3) the order of Creation; and, (4) the Fall of man in Eden.

Woman's Dress in Public

In 1 Corinthians 11:5 Paul says "Any woman who prays or prophesies with her head unveiled dishonors her head . . . ."

In 1 Timothy 2:8, 9 Paul says "I desire . . . that women should adorn themselves modestly and sensibly in seemly apparel, not with braided hair or gold or pearls or costly attire . . . ."

In 1 Peter 3:3, 4 Peter exhorts wives, "Don't be concerned about the outward beauty that depends on jewelry, or beautiful clothes, or hair arrangements. Be beautiful inside, in your hearts, with the lasting charm of a gentle and quiet spirit which is so precious to God" (LB).

When we look at the context of these passages (including 1 Corinthians 11:5), it is obvious that Paul and Peter must have had in mind the extreme patterns of dress used by prostitutes of the New Testament world. They wore "outlandish" hairdos, including false hair and wigs. They used elaborate jewelry and extravagant, excessive, and immodest dress. Some of the new women converts—fresh out of pagan society—were continuing some of these dress habits of their pre-Christian days in the worship services. These three passages are designed to protect these new converts from undue criticism. The passages do not call for complete abstinence from wearing jewelry, wigs, or fine clothing. They insist that a woman's purpose in the Christian life was not to emphasize outward appearance—external and physical beauty—but rather it was to emphasize her personality and her inner beauty. True beauty is from within and is a gentle, charming, spiritual beauty reflecting the values that are precious in God's sight. (Note that there is nothing in these passages that calls for female subservience!)

Woman's Silence in Worship Services

There are very few people who are not familiar with the fact that the Bible says, "The women should keep silence in the churches" (1 Corinthians 14:34). Yet most people have no idea where the statement is located in the Scriptures. Few people have made an effort to make a careful study of the passage in order to determine its real meaning. In this passage (verses 34, 35), Paul writes, "Let your women keep silence in the churches: for it is not permitted unto them to speak . . . if they will learn anything, let them ask their husbands at home: for it is a shame for women to speak in the church" (KJV).

It is true that some women were required to keep silence in the Jewish synagogue. Since Paul allowed women to pray and prophesy (1 Corinthians 11:5), it is doubtful that all women were required to be silent in all the New Testament churches. Then what is the meaning of these two passages? We can probably find the answer in Paul's concern about specific situations in particular churches. For example, the Corinthian church had many complex problems within the membership. First Corinthians was a letter written by Paul in reply to a letter the church in Corinth had written to him, asking for help in solving their problems (1 Corinthians 7:1). In light of the basic principles set out in chapter 2, it is unthinkable that Paul would give a universal command that all women for all time should not speak in a church worship service! It is unthinkable that Paul would command Phoebe, Priscilla, Chloe, Lydia, and many others not to speak in a church worship service!

Obviously then, Paul was saying that certain women in this particular church, who were disturbing the worship services should keep silent. How were they disturbing the worship services? The disturbance may have been idle talk, chatter, and gossip. Could it be the letter, spoken of in 1 Corinthians 7:1 written to Paul (now lost) gave a description of some noisy women who refused to be silent? Or, could it be that the special situation was the extremes of certain women in the congregation who were speaking in tongues? Paul discusses in detail the problem of speaking in tongues in the churches (1 Corinthians 14:27–34). Dr. Herschel H. Hobbs says of this passage:

> Since this statement appears in the apostle's treatment of tongues, it seems to be that, women evidently were the main offenders. In the nearby Oracle of Delphi and in the Temple of Aphrodite on the Acrocorinthus, located 1,800 feet above Corinth, women priestesses in rituals worked themselves into

an ecstasy in which they uttered strange sounds. In the latter case, the women were used by men in worshipping the sex goddess. Paul said that if Christian women spoke in tongues publicly, people would regard them as the same kind of women.[36]

Whatever the reason for keeping silent, 1 Corinthians 14:34 and 1 Timothy 2:11, 12 should not be interpreted as a universal command to women. The many Bible passages that are positive in theology and doctrinal in context should be used to interpret passages describing isolated practical personal problems and customs of the day.

One must not overlook the fact Paul did not hesitate to silence some men in a particular situation. They were counterfeit Christians who were disrupting the worship and teachings of a church (probably in Crete), where Titus was pastor. Note the bitter and severe language Paul uses in encouraging Titus to silence these men: "For there are many insubordinate men, empty talkers and deceivers, especially the circumcision party; they must be silenced, since they are . . . teaching for base gain what they have no right to teach . . . . Therefore rebuke them sharply, that they may be sound in the faith" (Titus 1:10–13).

Does the Order of Creation Indicate Female Submission?

The advocates of hierarchy defend male authority and female subordination on the ground of the "order of Creation" of male and female as recorded in Genesis. They point out that God first created Adam out of the dust of the ground (Genesis 2:7), and then He afterwards created Eve out of one of Adam's ribs as a "help meet" for Adam (Genesis 2:20–22 KJV). The argument claims Adam was created first and that Eve was created second, and created out of Adam's rib; therefore this is evidence that husbands are to have final authority over their wives and that wives are to be submissive to their husbands. The statements concerning Adam and Eve's creation are correct, but the hierarchy interpretation of the biblical statements is highly debatable.

Some questions are in order. Does it follow that the time sequence of Adam and Eve's creation (Adam first and Eve second) universally determines the worth and value of husbands and wives, and their social roles? If so, then since animals were created before Adam, does this mean that animals should have authority over men?

In light of the facts that (1) God created lower forms of life first; (2) He created successively higher forms of life second (light, water, soil, plants, fish, birds, animals, people); and, (3) in the final act of Creation He created Eve. (If we follow the time-sequence argument,) would not Eve be considered the highest form of creation? She was the apex, the final act of God's Creation. Thus, Adam would be subordinate to Eve.

Therefore, are we not justified in concluding that the eternal values God places upon both men and women have no relation to the time sequence of the Creation? Their worth and value were determined in the mind of God when He created them both in His image.

Does it follow that because Eve was created from Adam's rib that wives should be submissive to their husbands? Such a conclusion is a first-class example of reading cultural tradition of male authority into the Scriptures. To imply that the stuff (dust and a rib) from which God created male and female determines the worth of each, sounds more like Greek philosophy (shades of Plato) than the Christian Scriptures. Could not our infinite Creator have created man and woman both out of dust, or a rib, or any other substance, or out of nothing if He wanted to? Really now, isn't dust or a rib of small or no importance in the majestic act of God's Creation?

Did not God go through the same process in creating Eve as when He created Adam? The Genesis record would so indicate. Was Eve created imperfect or subnormal? According to the Genesis record, she was not. Both Adam and Eve were created in God's image! Both were commanded to marry and become one flesh! Both were given authority over plant and animal life! They both were created members of the same species!

Does the fact that Eve was created as Adam's "help meet" (Genesis 2:18, 20 KJV) indicate that she should be submissive to Adam? The hierarchy advocates seem to say *yes*. *Does it?* The King James translation of *help meet* is another example of how male translators have read the tradition of male authority into their translations. Some people in quoting the passage call it *helpmate*. This further implies female submissiveness. What does the original Hebrew word mean in the context of Genesis 2? The Hebrew *ezer* is a noun meaning "helper" and *neged* is a preposition meaning "corresponding to" or "equal to." The Revised Standard Version translates it "a helper fit for him." The Amplified Bible translates it "a helper meet for him" but in parenthesis adds "suitable, adapted, completing" as other meanings included in the original word of the original language. The Living Bible translates it "a helper suited to" his needs. Thus the original Hebrew words in this context seem to mean that Eve was created as a person (in the same sense that Adam was created a person) to have fellowship with Adam, to meet his needs, to complete him. Note that immediately after the Genesis account of Eve's creation, there is the statement, "Therefore a man leaves his father and his mother and cleaves to his wife, and they become one flesh" (Genesis 2:24, 25). This seems to put men and women (husbands and wives) into marriage on equal levels of partnership. Thus, the effort to read male dominant and female subordinate roles into the King James Version *help meet* has to be rejected.

Does the Fall of Man in Eden Indicate Female Subordination?

Some hierarchy thinkers insist that the Fall in the Garden of Eden is biblical proof of woman's subordination. They quote Paul, "And Adam was not deceived, but the woman was deceived and became a transgressor" (1 Timothy 2:14). They assume Eve was weaker than Adam. They assume she was gullible, listened to Satan, and was the cause of the Fall of Man in the Garden of Eden.

Two statements from Paul seem to refute this assumption. "Wherefore, as by one man [Adam, mankind] sin entered into the world, and death by sin; and so death passed upon all men, for that all have sinned" (Romans 5:12 KJV); and "For since by man came death, by man came also the resurrection of the dead. For as in Adam [mankind] all die, even so in Christ shall all be made alive" (1 Corinthians 15:21, 22 KJV). Paul uses the terms "one man" and "Adam" in the generic sense, meaning "mankind."

If one lifts 1 Timothy 2:14 out of its context, as the hierarchy defenders do, it fits their theory. But what is the context of the passage? It concerns public worship in a church, including women's dress and women's silence in worship services. Could it be that in 1 Timothy 2:13, 14 Paul was trying to correct questionable behavior of women in a specific church as discussed above? This seems to be the case. To say that Paul was saying all women in all churches in all future generations should be submissive to their husbands because Eve sinned first in the Garden of Eden is to disregard and violate the thrust and force of the many positive basic doctrinal passages, already stated, that call for equality of man and woman.

Many also point to ". . . and he [husband] shall rule over you [wife]" (Genesis 3:16) as proof positive that God intended for the husband to exercise authority over the wife in all cultures for all time. Once again we must look at the passage from which this statement is taken. This is not a command from God, but a part of the curse on Adam and Eve because of their sin. We need to distinguish between a command and a curse. A command expresses God's ideal for mankind, whereas a curse states what will follow as a result of sin. Male domination is the result of his sinful nature and not a part of God's creative plan. It is significant that Genesis 3:16 is never quoted in the New Testament to justify male supremacy.

There are many other arguments set forth by the hierarchy thinkers in an effort to bolster female submission. Let us examine briefly a few of them.

Two Creation Accounts

It is obvious that those who defend the doctrine of female submission tend to avoid discussing certain passages related to the Creation and the Fall of Man, such as Genesis 1:27; 2:24; 5:1, 2; Romans 5:12–19; and 1 Corinthians 15:21, 22. At the same time they emphasize Genesis 2:18–23; 3:1–16. They seem to be more interested in the second account of Creation in Genesis 2 than the first account found in the first chapter. Their avoidance of the first account of Creation is not because they are afraid of the so-called conflict between the two passages, but rather it would appear that they prefer to avoid the concept of equality set forth therein.

In general, both the equality and the hierarchy thinkers feel that there is no major problem involved in the "so-called conflict" between the two accounts of Creation that are the favorite whipping boys of liberal criticism. Most of those on both sides would agree with Dr. L. R. Elliott, who, in discussing the two Genesis accounts, says:

> In 1:1–2:3 is the record of the origin of the physical creation—mineral, vegetable, animal, including man. The Creator is the Sovereign, Almighty God, and man is related to God only in the same way as the rest of the orders of creation. The Creator's name is the general all-inclusive term—God. In 1:1 "God created the heavens and the earth"; in 2:1 God finished the heavens and the earth "and all the host of

them." Man is a part of the "host"(sic)—not distinguished from it. The emphasis is on the total creation; man is incidental to it.

When we come to the second account, 2:4–25, the physical creation is incidental—only three verses, 4–6—and the emphasis is on man, nineteen verses, 7–25. Also, man is now seen in close, personal relations with his Creator, which was not so in the first account. Because of this personal relation, the creative activity became moral as well as physical. And, most important difference of all, the Creator is not only God, But "the *Lord* God." [37]

God Is Not Masculine

Some thinkers have justified the hierarchy doctrine by assuming that God is masculine. But there is no biblical evidence for this. God is neither masculine nor feminine. He has no gender. Jesus said to the Samaritan woman at the well at Sychar, "God is spirit, and those who worship him must worship in spirit and truth" (John 4:24). God is not human. He created humanity.

Equality of the Trinity

Other thinkers try to anchor the order of the family hierarchy in the assumed order of the Trinity of God the Father, God the Son, and God the Holy Spirit. It is assumed that the Son was subordinate to the Father and the Spirit was subordinate to the Son. This assumption is not only not in the Scriptures but is rejected by the Scriptures. Jesus said, "I and the Father are one" (John 10:30); and "He who has seen me has seen the Father . . . " (John 14:9).

A review of the Scriptures discussed in this Appendix, as well as in chapter 2, presents a strong case for the biblical support of husband-wife equality. It is difficult to overcome the misconceptions of generations, but the time to do so is now.

Source Notes

1. Larry Christenson, *The Christian Family* (Minneapolis: Bethany Fellowship, Inc., 1970) p. 17.
2. One source indicates that in 1970 the median income for women in the USA who worked outside the home was $5,440, while it was $9,184 for men. By now the gap is even wider.
3. William Owen Carver, *The Glory of God in the Christian Calling,* A study of the Ephesian Epistle (Nashville: Broadman Press, 1949), pp. 167, 168.
4. Nancy A. Hardesty, in a letter to the editor, *Christianity Today,* June 4, 1976, p. 25.
5. A paraphrase of Philippians 2:3, 4 (PHILLIPS).
6. James H. Olthuis, *I Pledge Thee My Troth* (New York: Harper & Row, Publishers, 1975), p. 36.
7. Elisabeth Elliot, *Let Me Be a Woman* (Wheaton, Illinois: Tyndale House Publishers, 1976), p. 131.
8. *Home Life.* A Christian Family Magazine, published monthly by The Sunday School Board of the Southern Baptist Convention, 127 Ninth Avenue, North, Nashville, Tennessee 37234.
9. Judson and Mary Landis, *Building a Successful Marriage,* Sixth Edition (Englewood Cliffs, New Jersey: Prentice-Hall, Inc., 1973), p. 290.
10. Paul Popenoe, *Sex, Love and Marriage* (New York: Belmont Books, 1963), pp. 116–18.
11. Christenson, *The Christian Family,* pp. 22, 23.
12. T. B. Maston, *Christianity and World Issues* (New York: Macmillan, Inc., 1957), p. 70.
13. Herbert J. Miles, *Sexual Understanding Before Marriage* (Grand Rapids: Zondervan Publishing House, 1970), pp. 165–170.
14. Gary Collins, *The Secrets of Our Sexuality* (Waco, Texas: Word, Inc., 1976), p. 57.
15. *Ibid.,* pp. 61–66.
16. Gladys Hunt, *MS Means Myself* (Grand Rapids: Zondervan Publishing House, 1972), p. 38.
17. Lou Beardsley and Toni Spry, *The Fulfilled Woman* (Irvine, California: Harvest House Publishers, 1975), p. 5.
18. Miles, *Sexual Understanding,* pp. 165–171.
19. Herbert J. Miles, *Sexual Happiness in Marriage* (Grand Rapids, Michigan: Zondervan Publishing House, 1967), pp. 82f.

20. *Ibid.*
21. Robert N. Butler and Myrna L. Lewis, *Sex After Sixty* (New York: Harper & Row, Publishers, 1976), p. 95.
22. Miles, *Sexual Understanding,* chapters 9 and 10.
22a. Lewis B. Smedes, *Sex for Christians* (Grand Rapids: William B. Eerdmans Publishing Company, 1976), p. 244.
23. Tim and Beverly LaHaye, *The Act of Marriage* (Grand Rapids, Michigan: Zondervan Publishing House, 1976), p. 275.
24. Shirley Rice, *Physical Unity in Marriage,* A woman's view (published by the Tabernacle Church of Norfolk, 7120 Granby St., Norfolk, Virginia 23505, 1973), p. 15.
25. Ed and Gaye Wheat, *Intended for Pleasure* (Old Tappan, New Jersey: Fleming H. Revell Company, 1977), p. 76.
26. LaHaye, *The Act of Marriage,* p. 276.
27. Daniel Cappon, *Toward an Understanding of Homosexuality* (Englewood Cliffs, New Jersey: Prentice-Hall, Inc., 1965), p. 302.
28. Paul Popenoe, ed., *Family Life,* monthly service bulletin of the American Institute of Family Relations (Los Angeles, September, 1974), p. 6.
29. Miles, *Sexual Happiness,* chapter 6.
30. Wheats, *Intended for Pleasure,* p. 117.
31. Harold H. Titus and Morris To. Keeton, *Ethics for Today,* Fifth Edition (New York: Van Nostrand Reinhold Company, 1973), pp. 164, 165.
32. William H. Masters and Virginia E. Johnson in association with Robert J. Levin, *The Pleasure Bond* (Boston: Little, Brown and Company, 1975), p. 268.
33. Derrick Sherwin Bailey, *The Mystery of Love and Marriage,* A study in the theology of sexual relation (New York: Harper & Row, Publishers, 1952), p. 52.
34. Paul K. Jewett, *Man As Male and Female* (Grand Rapids, Michigan: Wm. B. Eerdmans Publishing Co., 1975), pp. 137, 138.
35. Letha Scanzoni and Nancy Hardesty, *All We're Meant to Be* (Waco, Texas: Word, Inc., 1974), p. 205.
36. Herschel H. Hobbs, "Baptist Beliefs," *The Baptist Standard,* June 9, 1976, p. 13.
37. L. R. Elliott, *The Bible and Its Critics,* an unpublished manuscript, Fleming Library, Southwestern Baptist Theological Seminary, Fort Worth, Texas, pp. 74, 75. (Authors' Note: Although written for "the people in the pew," we consider this to be the most scholarly refutation of liberal theology we have seen. Doctor Elliott has detailed footnotes—198 in all—and a bibliography of 222 books. He had been head librarian for thirty-five years at Southwestern Baptist Theological Seminary. Doctor Elliott died before this excellent manuscript could be published.)

Suggested Reading List

Butler, Robert N., and Lewis, Myrna L. *Sex After Sixty*. New York: Harper & Row. Publishers, 1976.

Collins, Gary R., editor. *The Secrets of Our Sexuality*. Waco, Texas: Word, Inc., 1976.

Dobson, James. *What Wives Wish Their Husbands Knew About Women*. Wheaton, Illinois: Tyndale House Publishers, 1975.

Guernsey, Dennis. *Thoroughly Married*. Waco, Texas: Word, Inc., 1975.

Hancock, Maxine. *Love, Honor and Be Free*. A Christian woman's response to today's call for liberation. Chicago: Moody Press, 1975.

Hollis, Harry, Jr. *Thank God for Sex*. Nashville: Broadman Press, 1975.

Hunt, Gladys. *MS Means Myself*. Being a woman in an uneasy world. Grand Rapids, Michigan: Zondervan Publishing House, 1972.

Jewett, Paul K. *Man As Male and Female*. Grand Rapids, Michigan: Wm. B. Eerdmans Publishing Company, 1975. (Scholarly and rather heavy)

Landorf, Joyce. *Tough and Tender*. What every woman wants in a man. Old Tappan, New Jersey: Fleming H. Revell Company, 1975.

Miles, Herbert J. *Sexual Happiness in Marriage*. Revised. Grand Rapids, Michigan: Zondervan Publishing House, 1976.

Morgan, Marabel. *The Total Woman*. Old Tappan, New Jersey: Fleming H. Revell Company, 1973.

Petersen, J. Allan, editor. *The Marriage Affair*. Wheaton, Illinois: Tyndale House Publishers, 1971.

Scanzoni, Letha, and Hardesty, Nancy. *All We're Meant to Be*. Waco, Texas: Word, Inc. 1975.

Schaeffer, Edith. *What Is a Family?* Old Tappan, New Jersey: Fleming H. Revell Company, 1975.

Small, Dwight H. *Christian: Celebrate Your Sexuality*. Old Tappan, New Jersey: Fleming H. Revell Company, 1975.

Vincent, M. O. *God Sex and You*. Philadelphia: J. B. Lippincott Company, 1971.

Wheat, Ed and Gaye. *Intended for Pleasure*. Old Tappan, New Jersey: Fleming H. Revell Company, 1977.

Scripture Index